The *Active Reader*

Book 4

Linda Kita-Bradley

Grass Roots Press

Edmonton, Alberta, Canada
2010

The Active Reader – Book 4 © 2010 Grass Roots Press

The Active Reader – Book 4 is published by

Grass Roots Press
A division of Literacy Services of Canada Ltd.
www.grassrootsbooks.net

AUTHOR	Linda Kita-Bradley
PASSAGES	Contributing Writers: Rose Boll, Terry Barber
EDITOR	Pat Campbell
DESIGN	Lara Minja
LAYOUT	Susan Hunter
PILOTERS	Avril Lewis, Dianne Manuel, Barb Pottier, Linda Stewart, with a special thanks to Halifax Community Learning Network

ACKNOWLEDGEMENTS

We acknowledge the financial support of the Government of Canada through the Book Publishing Industry Development Program (BPIDP) for our publishing activities.

We acknowledge the support of the Alberta Foundation for the Arts for our publishing programs.

ISBN 978-1-926583-18-1

Printed in Canada

Contents

About this workbook   iv

PEOPLE: The Arts

Unit 1: Susan Aglukark   **1**

Unit 2: Bill Reid   **11**

RELATIONSHIPS: Conflict Resolution

Unit 3: Conflict Styles   **21**

Unit 4: Active Listening   **31**

HEALTH: Different Ways of Eating

Unit 5: Why Vegetarian?   **41**

Unit 6: Conscious Eaters   **51**

ENVIRONMENT: Climate Change

Unit 7: Global Warming   **61**

Unit 8: Melting Ice   **71**

HISTORY: A Land of Many Peoples

Unit 9: The Acadians   **81**

Unit 10: Settling the Prairies   **91**

Answer Key   **101**

About this workbook

Welcome to Book 4 of *The Active Reader* series. This workbook aims to engage learners in the process of active reading by (1) providing stimulating reading passages, thought-provoking discussion questions, and practical literacy activities, and (2) helping learners develop the skills and strategies to become independent readers.

The workbook is organized around five themes: people, relationships, health, the environment, and history. Each theme consists of two units that provide the following activities:

Pre-reading
Photos, cartoons, and discussion questions introduce learners to the unit topic, activate learners' background knowledge, personalize the unit topic, and provide a purpose for reading.

Main Reading Passage
Learners are encouraged to read actively through making inferences, visualizing, predicting, and making personal connections with the text. Sidebars explain vocabulary or provide additional information to enhance understanding of the text.

Post-reading
Learners discuss questions that provide further practice making inferences and personal connections with the text as well as summarizing ideas, drawing conclusions, and working with main ideas. Learners are also encouraged to think beyond the text through relating key ideas and themes from the passage to current trends and events.

Vocabulary
Learners deepen their understanding of target vocabulary by producing the vocabulary in discussion and writing.

Dictionary Use
Learners are introduced to the parts and functions of a dictionary entry. This knowledge acts as a base for activities that guide the learners through the process of thinking about the meanings of words in context and choosing appropriate definitions from sample dictionary entries.

Mini-Lesson
Learners focus on making inferences, forming opinions, finding main ideas, and recognizing text structures.

Literacy Practice
Learners are encouraged to engage in daily literacy practices through reading, analyzing, and discussing print forms such as graphs, ads, nutrition labels, surveys, and maps.

Word Attack
Learners attend to the structure of words as well as using syllabication to divide long words into "conquerable" parts.

© CP Images 2007

People
Susan Aglukark

Vocabulary: despair   lobby   inspiration

Mini-Lesson: Making Inferences

Literacy Practice: Bar Graph

© www.CartoonStock.com/Ronaldo Dias

▶▶ Discussion

Have you ever sung in public?
        Describe your experience.

Who are your favourite singers?
        Why do you like them?
        What do you know about them?
        What do they sing about?

Susan Aglukark is an Inuit singer who
writes songs about her personal life.
Why do you think Susan sings about her
personal life? Write your ideas here.

_____

_____

_____

_____

Read the passage to find out how writing
songs has helped Susan.

Susan Aglukark

Susan grew up in Nunavut with her Inuit family. Her father was a Christian minister. Susan sang and played guitar in the church choir. After high school, she started singing in local communities. Her voice was not trained and she could not read music. Susan loved to sing but never dreamed music would be her career.

In the fall of 1990, a radio producer in Ottawa heard Susan sing. He knew she had talent. Susan started to record her music. Within five years, Susan's song *O Siem* was number one in Canada. Soon, she began winning major music awards.

© CP Images 2007

Stop and Think:

**Imagine you are Susan.
How does your life change once you are famous?**

Susan sings about her life. Susan was sexually abused at age nine. Her song *Still Running* is about sexual abuse. Some of Susan's relatives killed themselves. She sings about the **despair** that leads people to commit suicide. Susan also sings about the problems related to alcohol and drugs. Susan faces these painful truths with courage. Her music offers hope to Inuit people.

> **O Siem:** (oh-see-EM) Inuk word for "joy in community"

Stop and Think:

How does music affect you?

Susan does more than just sing out. She speaks out. She travels the north to talk to young people. She talks about social issues in their community. She volunteers with groups that help youth at risk in big cities. She gives self-esteem workshops. Susan also teaches Native Studies in a university. She acts as a mentor to

> **mentor:** a person that we trust to guide or advise us

student artists on campus. And Susan **lobbies** the government to support Aboriginal students so they can earn a degree.

Susan finds it hard to balance her responsibilities.

Stop and Think:

What responsibilities do you think Susan has? Read on to see if your ideas match the passage.

Susan is married and has a teenage son. She lives in Ontario but stays in touch with her family and friends in Nunavut. She works on her career as a singer and songwriter. Susan's faith is important to her. She prays daily and does not smoke or drink. She finds it difficult to make enough time for everything. "Everyone is born with the tools needed to cope with life," Susan says. "Each of us must learn how to use those tools for ourselves."

Susan is a role model for all people. Her strength and love of community are an **inspiration** to everyone. As she says in O *Siem*, "We are all family."

· · · · · · · · · · · · · · · · · · ·

Check the ideas you wrote on page 1 about Susan Aglukark. Can you find your ideas in the passage?

If not, do your ideas connect in some way to the ideas in the passage? How?

role model: a person who we imitate because we want to be like them

▶▶ Discussion

1. Susan says, "Everyone is born with the tools needed to cope with life." Susan's tools include her music, faith, community, and family. What tools do you use to cope with life's challenges?

2. How do we know that music has been a major part of Susan's life?

3. How does Susan show her love for the Inuit people?

4. Why do you think faith became an important part of Susan's life?

5. Every community faces social issues that it must try to solve. What social issues does your community face? How do communities try to solve social issues?

Vocabulary

Circle the best meaning for each bolded word.
Figure out what the word means by looking at how it is used in the sentence.

1. For years, the woman tried to find her real mother. She finally gave up, but her feelings of **despair** never went away.
   (a) satisfaction
   (b) not wanting to live alone
   (c) not caring
   (d) loss of hope

2. Our MP **lobbies** the government to spend more money on daycare. She emails reports to the leaders of every political party at least once a week.
   (a) pays a lot of money to
   (b) tries to affect decisions of
   (c) listens carefully to
   (d) tells lies about

3. The work he does for our community is an **inspiration** to me. Because of him, I became a social worker.
   (a) strong encouragement
   (b) big problem
   (c) something that is hard to understand
   (d) reason to fail

Write an answer for each question. Use complete sentences.

1. List one positive way and one negative way to cope with **despair**.

   _____

   _____

2. What do you want to make better in your community? Why? How would you **lobby** your local government to make it better?

   _____

   _____

3. Who has been an **inspiration** to you? How did this person affect you?

   _____

   _____

Dictionary Use

The act of reading involves the discovery of new words. Active readers use different strategies to understand vocabulary. What strategies do you use? Do you

> ask someone for the meaning of the word,
> guess the meaning, or
> skip the word?

Or do you use a dictionary? A dictionary gives the definition of words. What other information does a dictionary give about words? Write your answers on the lines.

_____   _____   _____

Here is some information that a dictionary provides.
Does the information match your ideas above?

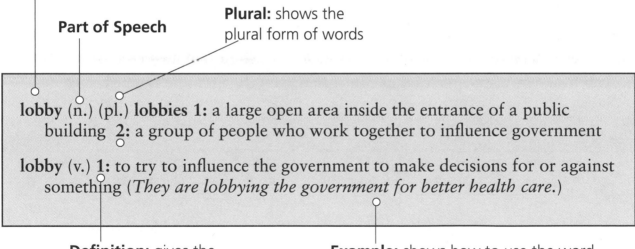

Main Entry

Part of Speech

Plural: shows the plural form of words

lobby (n.) (pl.) **lobbies 1:** a large open area inside the entrance of a public building **2:** a group of people who work together to influence government

lobby (v.) **1:** to try to influence the government to make decisions for or against something (*They are lobbying the government for better health care.*)

Definition: gives the meaning of the word

Example: shows how to use the word

Use the dictionary entry for *lobby* to answer the following questions:

1. How many definitions for *lobby* are in the dictionary entry? _____
2. Circle the parts of speech for *lobby.* noun (n.)   verb (v.)   adjective (adj.)
3. Circle the correct spelling of the plural for *lobby*: lobbis   lobbies   lobbeys
4. How many examples does the dictionary entry have for the word *lobby*? _____

Mini-Lesson: Making Inferences

What is an inference?

Sometimes, the writer does not tell the reader everything. Readers make an inference when they try to figure out the writer's hidden message or meaning.

How do we make inferences?

Active readers use their experience and knowledge to make an educated guess about hidden messages or meanings. Readers who make inferences **use the clues in the text together with their own experiences** to help them figure out the hidden messages.

We make inferences every day. Imagine that you see heavy, black clouds in the sky. You can make the inference, or educated guess, that it is going to rain. How can you make this inference? Because you already know from past experience that heavy, black clouds often produce rain.

Look at the chart below. Make one inference for each of the observations. Explain how you were able to make the inference. The first one is an example.

Observation	My inference
There are heavy, black clouds in the sky.	*I think there's a good chance it will rain because I know black clouds often produce rain.*
1. A seven-year-old boy comes home from school crying.	*I think*
2. A car alarm goes off late at night.	*I think*

Read what the writer says about Susan Aglukark.
Make an inference. Explain how you were able to make the inference.
The first one is an example.

Text	My inference
Susan's voice was not trained and she could not read music.	*I think Susan had a lot of natural talent because she became famous even without music lessons.*
1. Susan loved to sing but never dreamed music would be her career.	*I think*
2. Susan volunteers with groups that help youth at risk.	*I think*
3. Susan lobbies the government to support Aboriginal students so they can earn a degree.	*I think*
4. Susan lives in Ontario but stays in touch with her family and friends in Nunavut.	*I think*

Literacy Practice: Bar Graph

Graphs show a lot of information, or data, using few words. We use bar graphs to show and compare data. When reading a bar graph, we must pay attention to the title, the two axes, and the bars. The bars represent the data.

Use the bar graph below to answer the questions on the next page.

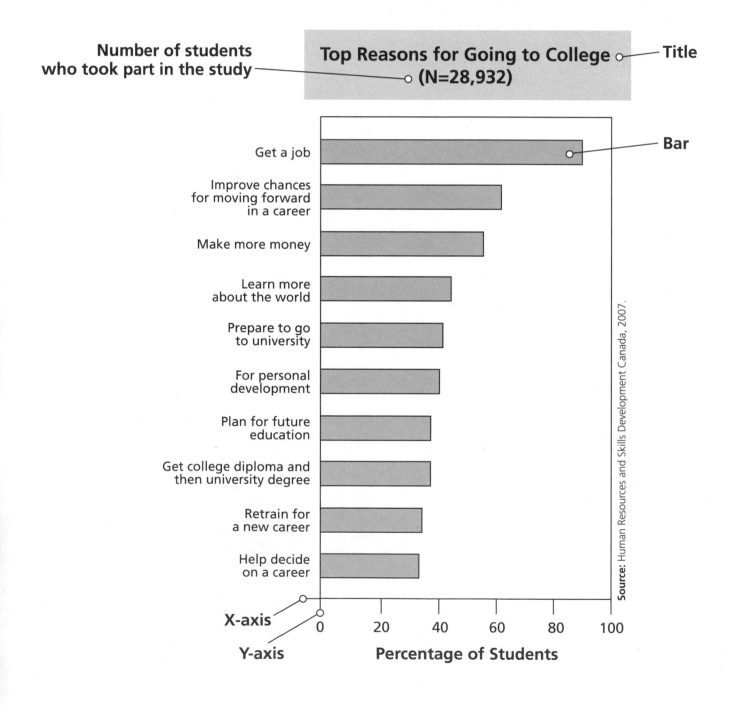

1. What is the title of the bar graph? _____

2. How many students took part in the study? _____

3. How many bars are there? _____ What do the bars represent?

   _____

4. How are the bars organized?

   _____

5. The Y-axis shows the reasons students go to college. What does the X-axis show?

   _____

6. Who collected the data?

   _____

7. When did they collect the data?

   _____

8. How do you think they collected the data?

   _____

9. Do you believe all the data in this bar graph? Why or why not?

   _____

Complete the sentences with data from the bar graph.

10. The most common reason for going to college is _____ .

11. The least common reason for going to college is _____ .

12. About _____ percent of students go to college to make more money.

13. About _____ percent of students go to college to learn more about the world.

14. About _____ percent of students go to college for personal development.

15. Why do you think upgrading skills is important?

   _____

Word Attack

Read the paragraph.
Circle six more words that have a suffix.

Susan grew up in Nunavut with her Inuit family. Her father was a (Christian) minister. Susan sang and (played) guitar in the church choir. After high school, she started singing in local communities. Her voice was not trained and she could not read music. Susan loved to sing but never dreamed music would be her career.

Suffixes

Many words have more than one part. They have a base word and an end part.

Christ   Christ**ian**
play   play**ed**

The end part is called a **suffix.**

Read the paragraph.
Circle three more compound words.

Susan works on her career as a singer and (songwriter.) She finds it difficult to make enough time for everything. "Everyone is born with the tools needed to cope with life," Susan says. "Each of us must learn how to use those tools for ourselves."

Compound Words

Compound words are made from two or more little words. **Songwriter** is an example of a compound word.

Read the sentences.
Divide the bolded words into parts.

Susan **volunteers** with groups that help youth at risk.

Susan finds it hard to balance her **responsibilities.**

Susan's strength is an **inspiration** to many.

Divide and Conquer

Some words are hard to read because they are long. It is easier to read long words if you divide them into parts.

For example,

community   com / mu / ni / ty

© CP Images 2007

People
Bill Reid

Vocabulary: overwhelm   stunning   figure

Mini-Lesson: Making Inferences

Literacy Practice: Graffiti

© www.CartoonStock.com/J.C. Duffy

"I don't know art, but I know what I like."

▶▶ Discussion

Paintings are one type of art. Look at the following list. In your opinion, which of these things represent art? Explain your answers.

calendar photos of a sunset
someone's doodle of a face
a sculpture of a cow in front of a building

Bill Reid was a famous First Nations artist. He carved sculptures that showed the life of Haida people. What kinds of things do you think Bill sculpted? Write your ideas here.

_____

_____

_____

Read the passage to find out about Bill's sculptures.

Bill Reid

As a young boy, Bill Reid always liked small things. He carved miniature tea sets from sticks of chalk. He painted the tiny teapots, cups, and saucers with nail polish. Canada's most famous First Nations artist also carved his first totem pole from a piece of chalk.

© CP Images 2007

Stop and Think:

What does this paragraph tell us about Bill's character as a boy?

Bill Reid was born on Canada's west coast in 1920. His father was American and his mother was Haida. In 1948, Bill moved to Ontario to study how to make jewellery. Three years later, Bill moved back to Vancouver and opened a small jewellery workshop. He made jewellery with modern European designs. Then, on a 1954 trip to *Haida Gwaii*, Bill saw a pair of bracelets that his great-uncle had carved. The beauty of the bracelets **overwhelmed** Bill. "The world was not the same," he said. From then on, Bill studied Haida designs. He made **stunning** jewellery by blending Haida and modern designs.

miniature: much smaller than actual size

Stop and Think:

Bill's world changed when he saw the Haida bracelets. Has an event in your life ever "changed your world"? Describe your experience.

Haida Gwaii (HI-duh-GWI): name for the group of islands off the coast of British Columbia

The Haida carved totem poles from huge cedar trees that grew along the coast. They carved human and animal **figures** such as the bear, wolf, frog, beaver, and whale into the poles. Some totem poles reached up to 30 m (100 ft) in height. Bill spent the late 1950s repairing totem poles and carving new ones. Bill's dream was to show the world the treasures of Haida culture. He started making large sculptures.

Bill took two years to carve *The Raven and the First Men* from a large block of yellow cedar. The huge sculpture tells the story of creation. Bill also carved a 15-metre (50-foot) war canoe. He painted a killer whale on the side of the canoe and named it *Lootaas*. Bill believed the Haida's greatest invention was the canoe.

The *Spirit of Haida Gwaii* is Bill's most famous sculpture. The sculpture is a 6-metre (20-foot) canoe carrying 13 figures from Haida stories and legends. Bill said, "The boat moves on, forever anchored in the same place."

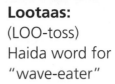

Lootaas:
(LOO-toss)
Haida word for "wave-eater"

Bill made two bronze copies of *The Spirit of Haida Gwaii* called *The Black Canoe* and *The Jade Canoe*.

Stop and Think:

How is it possible to move forward yet stay in the same place?

Bill died in 1998. But Canadians can see his art every day—on the back of the Canadian $20 bill.

. . . .

Check the ideas you wrote on page 11 about Bill Reid.
Can you find your ideas in the passage?
> If not, do your ideas connect in some way to the ideas in the passage? How?

▶▶ Discussion

1. Bill made sculptures that reflect his culture. Imagine you are a sculptor. What sculpture would you make to reflect your family? Your country? Explain your answers.

2. What events in Bill's life helped him grow as an artist?

3. How do we know that Bill was proud of the Haida culture?

4. Why do you think Bill's art is shown on the back of a Canadian bill?

5. Art is an optional subject in many junior high and high schools. Do you think art should be an optional or a required subject? Give reasons for your opinion.

Vocabulary

Circle the best meaning for each bolded word.
Figure out what the word means by looking at how it is used in the sentence.

1. Having too much work at one time **overwhelms** me. I don't like it.
   - (a) makes life boring for
   - (b) calms and relaxes
   - (c) takes over thought or feeling
   - (d) satisfies

2. The sunset was **stunning**. I stared at the changing colours for what seemed like hours.
   - (a) not interesting
   - (b) nice
   - (c) short and quick
   - (d) more than beautiful

3. I buy this cereal because my son collects the **figures** that come in each package.
   - (a) little statues of people or animals
   - (b) healthy food
   - (c) instructions for how to use
   - (d) stale pieces of something

Write an answer for each question. Use complete sentences.

1. Some events in life, such as having a baby, **overwhelm** people. What other events can overwhelm people?

   _____

   _____

2. Models in beauty magazines are often **stunning**. What makes the models look so beautiful in these magazine ads?

   _____

   _____

3. Some places, like McDonald's, give away action **figures** to children. Do you think this advertising strategy works? Why or why not?

   _____

   _____

Dictionary Use

Use the dictionary entries for *figure* and *stunning* to answer the questions below.

---

figure (n.) **1:** the shape or form of people or animals **2:** a symbol that represents a number *(The figures added up to an even one hundred.)*

figure (v.) **1:** to expect or think *(I figured you would be late.)* **2:** to calculate *(figure the cost)*

HINT: See page 5 if you need help to answer the questions.

1. How many definitions for *figure* are in the dictionary entry? _____
2. Circle the parts of speech for *figure*. noun (n.)   verb (v.)   adjective (adj.)
3. How many examples does the dictionary entry have for *figure*? _____

The dictionary entry for *figure* does not show the plural form. This is because the plural form is easy to spell. Just add *s—figures*.

---

stunning (adj.) **1:** very beautiful or pleasing **2:** very surprising or shocking *(The news about her mother was stunning.)*

---

4. How many definitions for *stunning* are in the dictionary entry? _____
5. Circle the part of speech for *stunning*. noun (n.)   verb (v.)   adjective (adj.)
6. Underline the example for *stunning*. What might the news be?

_____

Mini-Lesson: Making Inferences

Making an inference means using text clues and your own experiences to figure out the writer's hidden messages.

Read what the writer says about Bill Reid.
Make an inference. Explain how you were able to make the inference.
The first one is an example.

Text	My inference
Bill moved to Ontario to study jewellery-making.	*I think Bill moved to Ontario because there were more opportunities to study jewellery-making.*
1. Bill painted tiny teapots, cups, and saucers with nail polish.	*I think*
2. Bill moved back to Vancouver.	*I think*
3. Bill's dream was to show the world the treasures of Haida culture.	*I think*
4. Bill took two years to make *The Raven and the First Men* from a large block of yellow cedar.	*I think*

Read the following paragraph.
The underlined sentence contains a hidden message.
Possible inferences about the hidden message are written below the paragraph.

The First Tattoo

In 1991, the body of a man was found in Italy. The body was buried in the frozen earth. The body was over 5,000 years old. <u>Experts found 57 tattoos on the man's body including a cross on one knee.</u> Experts say the man suffered from arthritis. Experts believe the man got tattoos to cure his arthritis.

Possible inferences:

I think the man was religious because he had a tattoo of a cross.

I think the man believed in the healing power of tattoos because he had 57 tattoos.

I think the experts were scientists.

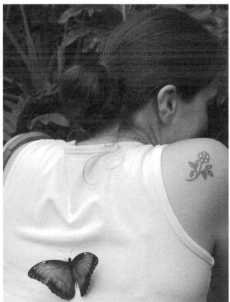

Read the following story.
The underlined sentence contains a hidden message.
Write your inference about the hidden message on the line below the paragraph.

Jen's Tattoo Story

I went and got my first and only tattoo for my 35th birthday last year. The flower reminds me of my grandmother, who died last year. My grandmother adored flowers. <u>She had flowers in her garden all year long.</u>

After my grandmother passed away, my family would say every time it rained that Gran was watering her flowers. This is why I wanted a flower tattoo.

Possible inference: _____

_____

Literacy Practice: Graffiti

Everyone has seen graffiti on walls, buildings, and bridges. Some people think graffiti is art; others think grafitti is vandalism. Graffiti artists create graffiti for many reasons: as a form of art, to entertain, to express an emotion, or to send a message.

Look at this sample of graffiti. Answer the questions below.

"One death is a tragedy a thousand is a statistic"

1. What images do you see in the graffiti? _____

2. What do the words mean? _____

   _____

3. Why did the graffiti artist create this graffiti?

   _____

4. How does the graffiti make you feel? Why?

   _____

5. What message does the graffiti artist want to send about society?

   _____

6. Which groups of people in society could identify with this graffiti?

   _____

▶▶ Discussion

Analyze the two samples of graffiti by discussing the following questions:

1. What does the graffiti mean to you?

2. How does the graffiti make you feel?

3. What message does the graffiti artist want to send?

4. Which groups of people in society could identify with the graffiti?

"Nobody cares"

And what do you think?

Vandalism, including graffiti, costs tax dollars, drives down the value of property, and leads people in the community to fear an increase in crime.

Source: *The Observer*, Sarnia, Ontario, posted October 3, 2009.

Word Attack

Read the paragraph.
Circle ten more words that have a suffix.

The Haida (carved) totem (poles) from huge cedar trees that grew along the coast. Bill spent the late 1950s repairing totem poles and carving new ones. Bill's dream was to show the world the treasures of Haida culture. He started making large sculptures.

Suffixes

Many words have more than one part. They have a base word and an end part.

carve   carve**d**
pole   pole**s**

The end part is called a **suffix.**

Read the paragraph.
Circle the compound word.

Bill moved to Ontario to study. Three years later, Bill moved back to Vancouver and opened a small jewellery workshop. He made jewellery with modern European designs.

Compound Words

Compound words are made from two or more little words.

Read the sentences.
Divide the bolded words into parts.

Bill carved **miniature** tea sets.

He made jewellery with modern **European** designs.

Canadians can see Bill's art every day.

Divide and Conquer

Some words are hard to read because they are long. It is easier to read long words if you divide them into parts.

For example,

jewellery   jew / ell / er / y

Relationships

Conflict Styles

Vocabulary: value   compromise   collaborate

Mini-Lesson: Forming Opinions

Literacy Practice: Advice Column

▶▶ Discussion

What do you think of when you hear the word *conflict*?

A conflict is a disagreement between two or more people.

> What kinds of things do people disagree about?

There are positive and negative ways to handle conflict. Think of positive ways to handle conflict. Write your ideas here.

_____

_____

_____

_____

Read the passage to find out the different ways people handle conflict.

Conflict Styles

Like snowflakes, no two people are alike. Each of us has our own ideas about the world and our place in it. Even in close relationships, the other person might not share all of our **values** and beliefs. Disagreeing on all sorts of things is normal. We disagree on how to raise children or who should do the laundry. We handle these disagreements, which are called conflicts, in different ways.

© iStockphoto/Peter Finnie

Stop and Think:

**Think about a time that you disagreed with someone.
How did you handle the conflict?
How did the conflict make you feel? Why?**

There are five common conflict styles. Do any of these styles describe how you handle conflict?

1. Walk Away: I prefer not to argue, so I walk away or keep quiet. I withdraw when I need time and space to think about the issue. But when I avoid the problem too often, I feel powerless and angry.

I'm sorry.

2. Your Way: I want my partner to be happy, so I give in. I end the argument to keep the peace. I do not mind giving in when the problem is not important to me. But, if I give in every time, I am ignoring my own needs. I begin to feel angry with my partner.

3. My Way: I know I am right, so I don't want to waste my time listening to my partner. I speak my mind and stand my ground. Sometimes, I lose my temper and yell, but this frightens my partner and we end up arguing more.

© Illustrations by Val Lawton

4. Half Way: I listen to my partner. Then we talk and try to reach a **compromise**. We both give up something, but meeting halfway can be just a quick fix to prevent an argument. We might miss a chance to work out a better solution.

5. Our Way: We both try to find a solution to the problem. We talk and listen to each other. It takes time and energy to **collaborate**, but in the end, we feel good. Two heads are better than one.

The way we respond to conflict can either help us or harm us. To keep relationships healthy, we must respond in ways that do not hurt either person. We must learn to make choices that turn conflict into a positive experience—a chance to grow and learn.

Check the ideas you wrote on page 21 about handling conflict. Can you find your ideas in the passage?

If not, do your ideas connect in some way to the ideas in the passage? How?

▶▶ Discussion

1. Think about two important people in your life. Match them to the conflict styles in the passage. Was it easy to match the people to the conflict styles? Why or why not?

2. Which conflict style is most positive? Explain your choice.

3. Reread the first three conflict styles. What leads to negative feelings in a conflict?

4. How do you think conflict can be turned into a positive experience?

5. Speaking one's mind is important. Yet, it is also important to listen to the other person. When should people speak their minds? What kinds of things block people from speaking their minds? How does being silenced make people feel?

Vocabulary

Circle the best meaning for each bolded word.
Figure out what the word means by looking at how it is used in the sentence.

1. He could have kept the wallet that he found. But because of his **values**, he returned the wallet to the owner.
   (a) greed and dishonesty
   (b) strong feelings of love
   (c) ideas about right and wrong
   (d) love of money

2. We finally came up with a **compromise**. I'm going to pay for his guitar lessons. He has to get a part-time job.
   (a) give-and-take solution
   (b) problem with no solution
   (c) argument
   (d) broken promise

3. Everyone in the community **collaborated** to solve the pothole problem. The city repaved our street last week.
   (a) gave up
   (b) refused
   (c) worked together
   (d) had a celebration

Write an answer for each question. Use complete sentences.

1. Different **values** are important to different people. For example, some people think being honest is more important than anything else. What are your most important values?

_____

_____

2. Describe the last **compromise** you made with someone. What did you give up to find a solution? What did the other person give up?

_____

_____

3. Sometimes it is good to work alone. Sometimes it is better to **collaborate**. Describe the last time you had to complete a project or make a decision. Did you work alone or did you collaborate with someone?

_____

_____

Dictionary Use

Do you remember what information a dictionary provides? A dictionary

> gives the definitions of a word,
> gives the parts of speech of a word,
> shows how to spell plural forms, and
> shows how to use the word.

Here is some other information a dictionary provides.

Syllables: divides the word into parts

Verb Forms: shows how to spell verb forms

col-lab-o-rate (v.) **collaborated; collaborating 1:** to work with another person or group in order to achieve or do something: COOPERATE **2:** to give help to an enemy who has invaded your country during a war *(He went to jail for collaborating with the enemy.)*

Synonym

Use the dictionary entry for *collaborate* to answer the following questions:

1. Why do you think it is a good idea to divide long words into syllables?

   _____

2. Cover the dictionary entry. Divide *collaborate* into syllables. _____

   Compare how you divided *collaborate* with the dictionary entry.

   Do you have to divide words in the same way as a dictionary?

   Why or why not? _____

3. Underline the two verb forms of *collaborate* in the dictionary entry.

   Fill in the blank below with the correct verb form of *collaborate*. Check your spelling.

   The two groups _____ and solved the problem.

4. Synonyms are words that have the same or similar meaning. Find and circle the synonym for *collaborate* in the dictionary entry.

Mini-Lesson: Forming Opinions

What is an opinion?

An opinion is a belief, judgment, or way of thinking about something. We often hold opinions even if it is hard to prove that they are 100 percent correct.

When do we form opinions?

Do you ever agree or disagree with something that someone says? Do you ever start an idea with the words "I think" or "I believe"? Do you ever question a politician's words?

If you answered "yes" to any of these questions, then you have formed opinions. Opinions are shaped by logic, knowledge, and experience. We form opinions every day on all kinds of issues from which brand of soup is best to how to raise children.

Active readers form opinions as they read. Active readers question what the writer says. They choose to agree or disagree with the writer's ideas. Sometimes readers have mixed feelings about an idea.

Read the following letter to an editor.
As you read, think about the following questions:

1. What are the effects of graffiti?

2. What does the writer think about graffiti?

(Re: The Underground Voice, Sept. 17) Last week five buildings downtown fell victim to graffiti. This is a sad event expected to cost $1,000 to clean up. And it makes the city look bad. I used to live in an area full of graffiti. Graffiti makes places look rundown. Some say that graffiti is a form of art. But most of the graffiti I see is not art. What happened downtown was simply a selfish form of cheap fun. There truly is no point to graffiti. It is simply the destruction of someone else's property. And it costs a lot of time and money to clean up! – *Edie Graff, Montreal*

Which of the writer's ideas do you agree with? Disagree with?
Which ideas do you have mixed feelings about?

The ideas below are from the passage *Conflict Styles*.
Do you agree or disagree with the ideas? Or do you have mixed feelings?
Complete the appropriate sentence(s).

1. Like snowflakes, no two people are alike.

   I agree because _____

   _____

   I disagree because _____

   _____

2. Disagreeing on all sorts of things is normal.

   I agree because _____

   _____

   I disagree because _____

   _____

3. Meeting halfway can be just a quick fix to prevent an argument.

   I agree because _____

   _____

   I disagree because _____

   _____

4. Two heads are better than one.

   I agree because _____

   _____

   I disagree because _____

   _____

Literacy Practice: Advice Column

Advice columns are found in newspapers, magazines, and on the Internet. Many advice columns are about relationships and money. Advice columns also cover topics such as health, pets, and taking care of plants.

The person who writes an advice column may be an expert. Or the advice may be based on personal experience. Many people read advice columns to get information. Others read advice columns for entertainment.

Ellie is a Canadian advice columnist.
Read Letter 1 to Ellie, and Ellie's advice.
Then answer the following questions:

1. Who is in conflict?

   _____

2. What does each person in the conflict want?

   _____

   _____

3. Which conflict style(s) do you recognize in the hairdresser?

   _____

4. Do you agree with Ellie's advice? Why or why not?

   _____

▶▶ Discussion

Read Letter 2 to Ellie, and Ellie's advice. Discuss the following questions:

1. Who is in conflict?

2. What does each person in the conflict want?

3. Which conflict style(s) do you recognize in the husband?

4. Do you agree with Ellie's advice? Why or why not?

Letter 1

My friend takes advantage of the fact I'm a hairdresser. She always begs me to cut her hair, saying she has no time for appointments. And she says that the salon where I work is too expensive.

I not only do it for free, but end up providing wine and dinner, since she turns the two-three hours into a social visit.

She's one of my few close female friends. But since she has a good job, I find this nervy and upsetting. Yet how do I stop a pattern that's been going on for a few years?

– *Scissors Friend*

Ellie's Advice to Letter 1

In a bad economy, we all must adapt. You can use logic to change how people act. And you need to insist on what you want.

Next time you chat, ask your friend how the bad economy is affecting her. (She is probably worried). Say that you're feeling the crunch, too, and need to make more money by cutting hair outside of work. Tell her how much you'll be charging and how eager you are for clients.

If your friend still begs for a free haircut, ask HER to bring the dinner and wine.

Letter 2

Me and my wife always argue. She never admits a mistake or takes responsibility in any conflict. I've apologized many times. She believes my way of thinking is wrong and doesn't believe in talking to a counsellor.

To her, I wasn't generous enough. Then, when I spend more money, the problem is I don't spend enough time with her.

After being at home more, she said, "You don't love me enough." How can I possibly make her happy? What am I doing wrong?

We're in our 40s and have no kids. We both work and have no money problems.

What are a man's duties toward his wife and what are the wife's?

– *Confused*

Ellie's Advice to Letter 2

Both of you have the same roles. You are partners and you both make money. So, you have the same responsibilities: 1) to respect each other and be sensitive to each other's needs; 2) to share tasks and expenses; 3) to work at the marriage.

You two seem 0 for 0 in this useless game of "Who's At Fault." You're both avoiding real communication, but in different ways. Your wife criticizes you constantly. You are defensive.

Face reality – there's no joy or point to this marriage unless you find out what's really going wrong. Maybe you don't express love other than to jump at her barking. Maybe she's unhappy for deeper reasons than you two have been willing to discuss.

Going to counselling may be your only hope for staying together. Tell her.

Word Attack

Read the paragraph.
Circle ten more words that have a suffix.

Each of us has our own (ideas) about the world and our place in it. Even in close (relationships), the other person might not share all of our values and beliefs. Disagreeing on all sorts of things is normal. We handle these disagreements, which are called conflicts, in different ways.

Suffixes

Many words have more than one part. They have a base word and an end part.

| idea | idea**s** |
| relation | relation**ships** |

The end part is called a **suffix**.

Read the paragraph.
Circle two compound words.

I listen to my partner. Then we talk and try to reach a compromise. We both give up something, but meeting halfway can be just a quick fix to prevent an argument.

Compound Words

Compound words are made from two or more little words.

Read the sentences.
Divide the bolded words into parts.

We talk and try to reach a **compromise**.

It takes time and energy to **collaborate**.

We must learn to make choices that turn conflict into a positive **experience**.

Divide and Conquer

Some words are hard to read because they are long. It is easier to read long words if you divide them into parts.

For example,

positive   po / si / tive

Relationships

Active Listening

Vocabulary: confirm   significant   establish

Mini-Lesson: Forming Opinions

Literacy Practice: Survey

▶▶ **Discussion**

Who do you think are better listeners?
Men? Women? Or are they equal?
     Explain your answer.

Good listeners are active listeners.
Active listeners give their full attention
to the speaker. Do you know any active
listeners? What kinds of things do they
say or do that show they are paying
attention to you? Write your ideas here.

_____

_____

_____

_____

Read the passage to find out what makes
a listener an active listener.

Active Listening

Have you ever started listening to someone speak, then find your thoughts starting to drift? Do you ever say, "Keep talking, I'm listening"? Then you carry on with some task, instead of giving the speaker your full attention? The speaker wants your attention. So the speaker feels upset or mad if you, the listener, are distracted.

Stop and Think:

How do you feel when someone does not listen to you?

We can avoid conflicts by being active listeners. Active listening means paying full attention to the speaker. Active listeners have a goal—to listen, to understand, and to **confirm** the speaker's meaning. How do active listeners reach their goal?

Active listeners...

1. focus on the speaker. They clear their minds of their own worries and concerns. They do not busy themselves with other tasks while listening.

2. are patient. Active listeners do not interrupt, even if they have a question.

3. do not judge the speaker, even if they do not agree with the speaker.

4. keep listening, even if they think the speaker's points are not relevant or interesting.

5. use body language to show they are listening. They maintain eye contact and nod to show attention. If sitting, active listeners lean forward.

Stop and Think:

What kind of body language do you use to show that you are listening?

6. notice the speaker's tone of voice and pace of words. Active listeners know that the way a person speaks gives clues to the speaker's feelings.

7. encourage the speaker to talk openly by saying, "Go on," or "Yes," or "I see."

8. make sure they understand the speaker's message. Active listeners ask questions and remember the answers. They say things like "Can you tell me more about...?"

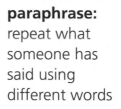

paraphrase:
repeat what someone has said using different words

9. confirm what the speaker means. Active listeners paraphrase the speaker's **significant** points. They say things like, "So you are saying that..." or "Do you mean that...?" Sometimes, active listeners use their own words to sum up the speaker's main points.

10. give feedback or advice, but only after thinking about the speaker's message. And only if the speaker asks for advice.

Stop and Think:

**Imagine you are pouring your heart out to a friend.
Your friend cuts in and gives you advice.
How do you feel? Why?**

Active listeners are involved listeners. Active listening can **establish** and build trust between the listener and the speaker. Active listeners benefit from improved relationships in all parts of their lives.

• • • • • • • • • • • • • • • • •

Check the ideas you wrote on page 31 about active listening.
Can you find your ideas in the passage?

   If not, do your ideas connect in some way to the ideas in the passage? How?

▶▶ Discussion

1. Think about conversations you have had with family, friends, or people at work. Do you spend most of the time speaking or listening? Do you sometimes find it hard to listen actively? Why?

2. What do active listeners pay attention to as they are listening?

3. Find three reasons why active listeners speak during a conversation.

4. In your opinion, why does active listening build trust between people?

5. Active listening is a good skill to have. In some jobs or positions, knowing how to listen actively is a must. What are some jobs or positions that require active listening? In *your* experience, how well do people in these jobs listen actively?

Vocabulary

Circle the best meaning for each bolded word.
Figure out what the word means by looking at how it is used in the sentence.

1. I called the dentist office to **confirm** the time of my appointment. Good thing!
   I thought my appointment was at 10:30 a.m. It's at 9:30 a.m.
   (a) make 100 percent sure   (b) change to make better
   (c) prepare in writing   (d) lie about

2. I write all **significant** dates, like birthdays and doctor appointments, on my calendar.
   (a) important   (b) easy to remember
   (c) once in a lifetime   (d) fun or entertaining

3. I was never able to **establish** a close relationship with my daughter. We respect each
   other. But we will never be friends.
   (a) prevent from happening   (b) understand clearly
   (c) create or start   (d) damage or break apart

Write an answer for each question. Use complete sentences.

1. Your power bill is going up every month, but you cannot explain why. What is one
   way to **confirm** that a mistake is not being made?

   _____

   _____

2. What is the most **significant** holiday of the year for you? Why is this holiday so
   important to you?

   _____

   _____

3. How can parents **establish** a positive relationship with their children?

   _____

   _____

Dictionary Use

Use the dictionary entries for *paraphrase* and *establish* to answer the questions.

> **par-a-phrase** (v.) **paraphrased; paraphrasing** to repeat what someone has said using different words: RESTATE *(I'm just paraphrasing. I can't remember every word he said.)*

HINT: See page 25 if you need help to answer the questions.

1. Long words are easier to spell if you write them syllable by syllable.

   Read each syllable of the word *paraphrase* in the dictionary entry.

   Cover the word. Say each syllable and write the word. _____

   Check your spelling.

2. Fill in the blanks with the correct verb form of *paraphrase*. Check your spelling.

   (a) I _____ the doctor's advice to make sure I understood.

   (b) Sometimes I leave out details when I'm _____.

3. Synonyms are words that have the same or similar meanings. Find and circle the synonym for *paraphrase* in the dictionary entry.

> **es-tab-lish** (v.) **1:** to create or start: SET UP **2:** to make the truth of something clear: PROVE *(establish a link between smoking and cancer)* **3:** to find out something *(The police established how the thief entered the house.)*

4. Read each syllable of the word *establish* in the dictionary entry.

   Cover the word. Say each syllable and write the word. _____

   Check your spelling.

5. How many definitions for *establish* have a synonym? _____

The dictionary entry for *establish* does not show verb forms because these verb forms are easy to spell. Just add *ed* or *ing*—*established* and *establishing*.

Mini-Lesson: Forming Opinions

The ideas below are from the passage *Active Listening*.
Do you agree or disagree with the ideas? Or do you have mixed feelings?
Complete the appropriate sentence(s).

1. We can avoid conflicts by being active listeners.

   I agree because _____

   _____

   I disagree because _____

   _____

2. The way a person speaks gives clues to the speaker's feelings.

   I agree because _____

   _____

   I disagree because _____

   _____

3. Give advice only if the speaker asks for advice.

   I agree because _____

   _____

   I disagree because _____

   _____

4. Active listeners benefit from improved relationships in all parts of their lives.

   I agree because _____

   _____

   I disagree because _____

   _____

Newspapers and magazines often have editorials.
Editorials are opinion essays.

Read the following editorial.
As you read, think about the following questions:

1. What do schools offer students?

2. What does the writer think schools should offer?

What are schools for anyway?

Schools used to teach mainly reading, writing and arithmetic. A little learning went a long way. But now, students need so much more. We want our children to have as many job options as possible after leaving school.

But we want our schools to be much more than job training centres. We also want schools to provide a classic education. We want our children to explore art, music, and drama.

We expect our schools to be daycare centres. Schools provide programs after school to keep our children safe until we pick them up. Schools have breakfast and lunch programs to keep our children's bellies full.

Schools teach our children values. They teach our children how to get along with others. They teach our children about respect, tolerance, and honest play. Schools are where our children learn about their bodies and how to make safe choices. Schools are where our children develop self-esteem.

Why are schools expected to provide so much more than just the basics? Maybe we, the parents, have not been doing our jobs as well as we should.

Do you agree or disagree with the writer's ideas? Or do you have mixed feelings?
Express your opinions by completing the following sentences.

I agree that _____ .

I kind of agree that _____ .

I don't agree that _____ *because*

_____ .

Literacy Practice: Survey

Researchers use surveys to gather information about people. Surveys consist of a list of questions. Researchers analyze the answers to the questions. They can then draw conclusions or form opinions.

Magazines often contain surveys. You can take the surveys and learn about yourself. Surveys cover topics from how healthy you are to how well you manage money to how sexy you are.

Many surveys in magazines are not based on science or research. People answer the questions and read the results just for fun.

Are You an Active Listener?

Take the following survey to learn if you are an active listener. Read each statement. Put a tick in the box that describes your behaviour.

Listening Skills	Never	Some-times	Often	Usually	Always
I clear my mind of personal worries before starting a conversation.					
I keep paying attention to the speaker even when the speaker talks for a long time.					
I focus on what the speaker is saying even when I do not think it is relevant.					
I listen to more than just the speaker's words. I try to understand how the speaker feels.					
I wait for the speaker to finish. Then I think about what I want to say.					

Listening Skills	Never	Some-times	Often	Usually	Always
I am comfortable with silence. I give the speaker time to think.					
If I don't understand, I ask the speaker to repeat or explain things.					
I don't finish the speaker's sentences.					
I don't interrupt, even if I think I know what the speaker is trying to say or going to say.					
I don't continue with other tasks while the speaker is speaking. All of my attention is on the speaker.					
I continue to listen, even if I don't agree with the speaker.					

Adapted from *Coach U personal and corporate coach training handbook*, (2005), page 134.

Are most of your answers "usually" or "always"?
If yes, you are probably a pretty good listener.

Are most of your answers "sometimes" or "never"? If yes, try this exercise:
    Review the skills that you marked "sometimes" or "never."
    Choose the skill that you think is the most important for active listeners.
    Practise this skill the next time someone needs you to be an active listener.

And what do you think?

What you say is important, but what you're doing while you say it is far more important. Body language conveys up to 93% of meaning.

Word Attack

Read the paragraph.
Circle eight more words that have a suffix.

(Active)(listeners) are involved listeners. Active listening can establish and build trust between the listener and the speaker. Active listeners benefit from improved relationships in all parts of their lives.

Suffixes

Many words have more than one part. They have a base word and an end part.

act   act**ive**
listen   listen**ers**

The end part is called a **suffix.**

Read the paragraph.
Circle two compound words.

Active listeners paraphrase the speaker's significant points. Sometimes, active listeners use their own words to sum up the speaker's main points. Active listeners give feedback or advice. But only if the speaker asks for advice.

Compound Words

Compound words are made from two or more little words.

Read the sentences.
Divide the bolded words into parts.

The speaker wants your **attention.**

Active listeners use body **language.**

Active listeners **encourage** the speaker to talk openly.

Divide and Conquer

Some words are hard to read because they are long. It is easier to read long words if you divide them into parts.

For example,

relevant   re / le / vant

© iStockphoto/Maksim Shmeljov

Health
Why Vegetarian?

Vocabulary: ethical   scarce   consume

Mini-Lesson: Finding the Main Idea

Literacy Practice: Nutrition Label

▶▶ **Discussion**

What do you know about vegetarian diets?

Why do you think some people become vegetarians? Write your reasons here.

_____

_____

_____

_____

Read the passage to find out why people choose to be vegetarians.

"So, that's 3 ham and cheese omelets ... one order without cheese, one without ham, and another without eggs."

© www.CartoonStock.com/Dan Reynolds

Why Vegetarian?

Vegetarians eat vegetables, right? Yes—plus a whole lot more. They eat fruits, grains, and seeds. Most vegetarians also eat dairy products and eggs. They do not eat the meat of animals, birds, or fish. Many people choose a vegetarian diet for health reasons. They believe vegetarians live long, healthy lives. People choose to be vegetarian for other reasons as well.

© iStockphoto/webphotographeer

Stop and Think:

Do you think a vegetarian diet is healthy?

Many people in North America are vegetarians for **ethical** reasons. They worry about cruelty to farm animals. Some giant meat companies operate large animal farms. These farms may contain 10,000 cows, 50,000 pigs, or 200,000 chickens. The animals are crowded into long barns and never see the sun. The barns are dirty and fresh air is **scarce**. The farmers inject drugs into the animals to make them grow faster. The animals suffer during their lives and when they are slaughtered. These farms produce meat much like a factory produces bricks. These farms are nicknamed "factory farms." Factory farms can make a lot of money, but they treat the animals badly.

> **slaughter:** kill an animal for food

Stop and Think:

How is a brick factory the same as a factory farm?

People also choose a vegetarian diet to help the environment. For example, a cow needs to **consume** six kg (13 lb) of grain to produce one kg (2.2 lb) of beef. But people could eat the grain instead of eating the beef. If people ate plants and grain instead of meat, more people could be fed using less land. We would not need to cut down our forests for pastureland. As a result, we would have more natural spaces for wildlife.

Stop and Think:

How many people could one kg of beef feed?
How many people could six kg of rice feed?

Factory farms are really bad for the environment. Growing one kg of beef creates 40 kg (88 lb) of manure. Growing one kg of pork creates 15 kg (33 lb) of manure. If this manure is not handled right, it can pollute our water both above and below ground. Also, factory farms use lots of fossil fuels such as oil and gas. Burning fossil fuels leads to global warming.

People make choices every day. Vegetarians believe a meatless diet is an ethical choice. Being vegetarian helps the environment. Being vegetarian helps farm animals. And being vegetarian might help end world hunger—all at the same time.

manure: animal body waste

fossil fuels: made from the remains of dead animals and plants. These fuels form over millions of years deep under the ground.

Check the ideas you wrote on page 41 about vegetarians.
Can you find your ideas in the passage?

> If not, do your ideas connect in some way to the ideas in the passage? How?

▶▶ Discussion

1. Would you consider becoming a vegetarian? Why or why not?

2. Which is better for the environment? Raising cows or pigs? Explain your answer.

3. Find four reasons why people would protest factory farms.

4. Why do you think some vegetarians do not eat dairy products or eggs?

5. Factory farms add to global warming by burning fossil fuels. What other human activities involve burning fossil fuels?

Vocabulary

Circle the best meaning for each bolded word.
Figure out what the word means by looking at how it is used in the sentence.

1. Should we use animals to test beauty products? This is an **ethical** question. The answer depends on a person's beliefs and experiences in life.
   (a) related to fashion
   (b) related to animal health
   (c) related to ideas of right and wrong
   (d) related to science and math

2. If clean water becomes **scarce**, our water bill will go up.
   (a) not enough
   (b) fresh
   (c) common
   (d) necessary

3. The United States could feed 800 million people with the grain that farm animals **consume**.
   (a) buy or trade
   (b) eat or use up
   (c) grow or raise
   (d) put in storage

Write an answer for each question. Use complete sentences.

1. Give one reason why a person might do something that is not **ethical**.

   _____

   _____

2. Quiet and relaxing places are becoming **scarce.** Do you agree? Explain your answer.

   _____

   _____

3. Some people love shopping. Why do some people **consume** so much?

   _____

   _____

Dictionary Use

**Read the following sentences. Write a synonym for the word *get*.
The first one is an example.**

(a) I *get* nervous when I have to speak in front of people. _____*become*_____

(b) I don't *get* what you mean. You're talking in circles. _____

(c) Did you *get* the birthday card that I sent you? _____

The main reason we use a dictionary is to find the definition of a word.
Many words, such as *get*, have more than one definition. You need to
read all the definitions in a dictionary entry. Then choose the one that
matches how the word is being used.

**Use the dictionary entry to find the definition of the bolded word in each sentence.
Write the number of the definition beside each sentence.
The first one is an example.**

---

con-sume (v.) consumed; consuming **1**: to eat or drink **2**: to use up *(consume gas, time, money)* **3**: to destroy with fire *(The files were consumed in the fire.)* **4**: to take all of a person's time and energy *(He was consumed with hate.)*

---

1. Cows and pigs **consume** a lot of grain. ___1___

2. She was so **consumed** by her work that she had no time to eat. _____

3. The apartment was totally **consumed** by fire. Luckily, no one died. _____

4. We need to **consume** less gas and oil. _____

5. She has a huge appetite. She can **consume** a whole chicken at one meal! _____

6. The divorce **consumed** most of his savings. _____

7. Don't let negative feelings **consume** you. Get on with life. _____

Mini-Lesson: Finding the Main Idea

Active readers look for the main idea as they read. The main idea is the most important idea in the paragraph. The main idea is stated in sentence form. It answers two questions:

What is the topic, or subject, of the paragraph?
example: vegetarian diet

What is the main point the writer makes about the topic?
example: A vegetarian diet is healthy.

Where do I find the main idea?

Look for the main idea in the first two or last two sentences of the paragraph.

How do I check the main idea?

Check to see if you have found the main idea by following these steps:

Step 1
Identify the topic in the main idea.

Step 2
Circle key words in the paragraph. Key words are the topic words and any synonyms for the topic words. For example, if the topic is animals, synonyms will include cows and pigs. If you have found the main idea, key words will appear many times in the paragraph.

Step 3
Find two or three details that support the main idea. If you have found the main idea, it will be easy to find supporting details.

**Look at the example on the following page.
The main idea is "Factory farms treat the animals badly."**

Many people in North America are vegetarians for ethical reasons. They worry about cruelty to farm animals. Some giant meat companies operate large animal farms. These farms may contain 10,000 cows, 50,000 pigs, or 200,000 chickens. The animals are crowded into long barns and never see the sun. The barns are dirty and fresh air is scarce. The farmers inject drugs into the animals to make them grow faster. The animals suffer during their lives and when they are slaughtered. These farms produce meat much like a factory produces bricks. These farms are nicknamed "factory farms." **Factory farms** can make a lot of money, but they **treat the animals badly.**

Step 1: Topic: animals in factory farms

Step 2: Key words: animal, cows, pigs, chickens, farm, factory

Step 3: Supporting details:
animals are crowded into long barns
animals never see the sun
barns are dirty
fresh air is scarce
farmers inject animals with drugs

**Read the paragraph. Choose the correct topic. Find the main idea.
Then check to make sure the main idea is correct.**

Experts do not agree on how much protein we should consume every day. But they do agree that protein is important. Like water, protein makes up a big part of the body. Protein helps build muscles, blood, skin, hair, and nails. It also builds organs like the heart and brain. Blood does not clot without protein. Protein helps our metabolism, and it helps our bodies fight off disease.

Topic: (a) blood   (b) protein   (c) water

Main Idea: _____

Supporting Details: _____

_____

_____

Literacy Practice: Nutrition Label

Nutrition labels help consumers make healthy food choices. The labels tell consumers what is in the food that they are buying. The labels contain information about vitamins, minerals, and nutrients. Iron and calcium are examples of minerals. Fat, sugar, and protein are examples of nutrients.

All packages of food must have nutrition labels. This is the law.

Look at the nutrition label for whole wheat bread. Where can you find information about the

(a) amount of fat _____

(b) amount of protein _____

(c) serving size _____

(d) amount of sugar _____

(e) number of calories _____

Put the correct number in the blanks.

Whole Wheat Bread

Nutrition Facts
Per 2 Slices (64 g)

Amount		% Daily Value
Calories 140		
Fat 1.5 g		2 %
Saturated 0.3 g + Trans 0.5 g		4 %
Cholesterol 0 mg		0 %
Sodium 290 mg		12 %
Carbohydrate 26 g		9 %
Fibre 3 g		12 %
Sugars 2 g		
Protein 5 g		
Vitamin A	0 %	Vitamin C 0 %
Calcium	4 %	Iron 10 %

1 — Per 2 Slices
2 — Calories
3 — Fat
4 — Sugars
5 — Protein

Peanut Butter

Nutrition Facts
Per 1 Tbsp. (15 g)

Amount		% Daily Value
Calories 90		
Fat 8 g		12 %
Saturated 1.5 g + Trans 0 g		8 %
Cholesterol 0 mg		0 %
Sodium 70 mg		3 %
Carbohydrate 3 g		1 %
Fibre 1 g		4 %
Sugars 1 g		
Protein 3 g		
Vitamin A	0 %	Vitamin C 0 %
Calcium	2 %	Iron 4 %

The chart below compares whole wheat bread and peanut butter.
Complete the chart by using the nutrition labels on page 48.

	Whole Wheat Bread	Peanut Butter (Kraft)
What is the **serving size**?		
How many **calories** are in the serving?		
How many grams (**g**) of **fat** are in the serving?		
How many grams of **protein** are in the serving?		

Use the information you found to answer the following questions:

1. Compare the numbers for whole wheat bread and peanut butter.
   Is one food item healthier than the other? If yes, how is it healthier?

   _____

   _____

2. How much protein does one peanut butter sandwich have? _____

3. Do you think it is healthy for a person to get all their protein from peanut butter sandwiches? Explain your answer.

   _____

   _____

And what do you think?

Nutrition labels are not exact. Canadian law allows for a 20% difference between real amounts of nutrients in a food and what a nutrition label says. If the label says 10 g of protein, for example, the food could really have 8 to 12 g of protein.

Even if nutrition labels are not exact, they are the best help consumers have when making food choices.

Word Attack

Read the paragraph.
Circle eight more words that have a suffix.

(Growing) one kg of pork (creates) 15 kg of manure.
If this manure is not handled right, it can pollute
our water both above and below ground. Also,
factory farms use lots of fossil fuels such as oil and
gas. Burning fossil fuels leads to global warming.

Read the paragraph.
Circle two compound words.

If people ate plants and grain instead of meat,
more people could be fed using less land. We would
not need to cut down our forests for pastureland.
As a result, we would have more natural spaces for
wildlife.

Read the sentences.
Divide the bolded words into parts.

All vegetarians eat **vegetables**. Most vegetarians
also eat dairy products and eggs.

People choose a vegetarian diet to help the
environment.

Protein helps our **metabolism**.

Suffixes

Many words have more than
one part. They have a base
word and an end part.

grow   grow**ing**
create   create**s**

The end part is called a **suffix.**

Compound Words

Compound words are made
from two or more little words.

Divide and Conquer

Some words are hard to read
because they are long. It is
easier to read long words if
you divide them into parts.

For example,

vegetarians ve / ge / tar / i / ans

Health
Conscious Eaters

Vocabulary: aroma   texture   savour

Mini-Lesson: Finding the Main Idea

Literacy Practice: Ad

▶▶ Discussion

Think about the last meal you ate. Describe *how* you ate the food.

To be conscious means to pay attention to what is happening at the moment.

How do you think conscious eaters eat? For example, would they sit down to eat or would they eat their food on the run? Write your ideas here.

_____

_____

_____

_____

Read the passage to find out about conscious eaters.

"Remember, chew every bite 32 times."

Conscious Eaters

Forget eating on the run. Forget fast food. Turn off the TV. Sit down. Slow down, and eat consciously. Conscious eaters believe paying attention to how they eat is just as important as paying attention to what they eat.

© iStockphoto/track5

Conscious eaters eat from plates and bowls, never from the box. They sit in a quiet place, perhaps with calm music or even a candle. Before starting the meal, conscious eaters focus with a moment of silence, or a prayer. They think about where their food comes from. They think about and quietly thank the farmers who grow the food, and the people who pick, package, and deliver it.

conscious:
(KAHN shus)

Stop and Think:

Do you think a lot of people have quiet meal times? Why or why not?

Conscious eaters eat slowly. They take small bites and chew the food many times to release the flavours. While they eat, conscious eaters take time to notice flavours such as sweet, salty, sour, and bitter. They notice the **aroma** of the food. They notice the **texture** of the food. Conscious eaters put down their fork and pause between mouthfuls. They **savour** the last bite of the meal. Then they sit back, relax, and take a deep breath. Conscious eaters do not let their minds race to other things they need to do or jump up from the table and busy themselves. They take a few moments to enjoy their feelings of satisfaction.

pause: stop for a period of time before starting again

Stop and Think:

Do you think a lot of people are conscious eaters? Why or why not?

Conscious eating is free. No expensive equipment or special foods are required. Over time, conscious eaters become healthier eaters because they think more carefully about their food choices. They experiment with and discover new foods. They try different spices or recipes, and find the time to cook more—or even bake. Conscious eaters sometimes lose weight because eating slowly allows them to notice when they are becoming full. Also, conscious eaters never eat just because they are bored or stressed. So conscious eaters do not overeat.

Stop and Think:

Why do you think conscious eaters try different foods and recipes?

Eating consciously is not a diet. It is a way of living. Some conscious eaters say meal times are the best part of their day. Try slowing down for one meal a day, or even one meal a week. Make time for yourself—and make the meal an event.

· · · · · · · · · · · · · · · ·

Check the ideas you wrote on page 51 about conscious eaters. Can you find your ideas in the passage?

If not, do your ideas connect in some way to the ideas in the passage? How?

▶▶ Discussion

1. Would you consider becoming a conscious eater? Why or why not?

2. Do conscious eaters spend a long time eating a meal? Explain your answer.

3. Find three possible benefits of being a conscious eater.

4. Why do you think conscious eating helps people to digest food better?

5. People's lives affect the way they eat. For example, busy people sometimes rely on fast food. What else affects people's eating habits and patterns?

Vocabulary

Circle the best meaning for each bolded word.
Figure out what the word means by looking at how it is used in the sentence.

1. The **aroma** of fresh-baked bread and spices filled the room when we opened up the pizza box.
   (a) soft feel
   (b) nice smell
   (c) high cost
   (d) loud noise

2. I like mashed potatoes that have a creamy **texture**.
   (a) how something smells
   (b) how something grows
   (c) how something is packaged
   (d) how something feels to the touch

3. I allow myself only one chocolate bar a week, so I **savour** each bite.
   (a) repeat many times
   (b) spit out quickly
   (c) forget after a short time
   (d) enjoy for as long as possible

Write an answer for each question. Use complete sentences.

1. **Aromas** sometimes bring back memories. What aromas, or smells, bring back memories for you?

   _____

   _____

2. Look around the room you are in right now. List the **textures** you can identify.

   _____

   _____

3. It is important to **savour** the special moments in life. What special moment do you remember in your life?

   _____

   _____

Dictionary Use

Use the dictionary entries to find the definition of the bolded word in each sentence.
Write the number of the definition beside each sentence.
The first one is an example.

> **di-gest** (v.) **1:** to break down food in the stomach and bowels **2:** to think over
> ideas and try to understand *(I couldn't digest the information. It came too
> fast.)* **3:** to treat a material with heat to break it down chemically *(digest
> wood pulp to make paper)*

1. Some people cannot **digest** milk products. __1__

2. The material needs to **digest** at a temperature of 150°C. _____

3. Stop! I need time to **digest** what you have just told me. _____

4. Cats can **digest** all types of things. _____

> **sa-vour** (v.) **1:** to enjoy the smell or taste of something for as long as possible
> **2:** to enjoy something for a long time *(savour good memories)*

5. I **savour** each day of summer! The winters are so long and cold. _____

6. People are too busy to cook. So they **savour** a home cooked meal. _____

Mini-Lesson: Finding the Main Idea

Quick Review

The main idea is the most important idea in the paragraph. The main idea answers two questions:

> What is the topic of the paragraph?
> What is the main point the author makes about the topic?

You can often find the main idea in the first two or last two sentences of the paragraph. You can check the main idea by

> finding the topic of the paragraph,
> circling key words, and
> finding supporting details.

Read the paragraphs. Choose the correct topic. Find the main idea. Then check to make sure the main idea is correct.

HINT: See page 46 to review the steps for checking main idea.

Paragraph 1

Conscious eaters eat slowly. They take small bites and chew the food many times to release the flavours. While they eat, conscious eaters take time to notice flavours such as sweet, salty, sour, and bitter. They notice the aroma of the food. They notice the texture of the food. Conscious eaters put down their fork and pause between mouthfuls. They savour the last bite of the meal. Then they sit back, relax, and take a deep breath. Conscious eaters do not let their mind race to other things they need to do or jump up from the table and busy themselves. They take a few moments to enjoy their feelings of satisfaction.

Topic:
(a) why people eat (b) how conscious eaters digest food (c) how conscious eaters eat

Main Idea: _____

Paragraph 2

Farmers across Asia and Africa grow rice. The farmers clear and plough the land. They divide the land into sections. Each section of land is bordered with a bank of soil. The land is flooded with water. Farmers plant the rice in the flooded field. They make a hole in the soil for each little rice plant. Planting takes hours and hours, often under a hot sun. The farmers harvest the rice with a knife. They cut the rice plants and tie them in bundles. The bundles of plants dry in the sun. Then the plants are smashed to separate the grains of rice from the plant. Finally, the grains of rice are picked out, by hand, from the pile of smashed rice plants. Growing rice is not easy work.

Topic: (a) farmers in Asia and Africa   (b) growing rice   (c) working in the hot sun

Main Idea: _____

Paragraph 3

Eating slowly helps your body digest food. Taking time to smell food is important. When you smell something good, your mouth starts to produce saliva. Saliva helps break down food as you chew. Chewing food slowly also helps your body digest food. The stomach does not have to work as hard to break down the food. And chewing food slowly gives your stomach time to produce enzymes. Enzymes help the stomach digest food. Finally, eating slowly helps your body know when your stomach is full. Your stomach will not become overloaded with food. As a result, your stomach can digest food more easily.

Topic: (a) digesting food   (b) chewing food   (c) keeping your stomach full

Main Idea: _____

Literacy Practice: Ad

Our lives are full of ads. We see ads on TV, in store windows, on billboards, and in magazines. We see ads on buses, telephone poles, and even in public washrooms. How do ads get our attention? How do ads convince us to buy the product?

Answer the following questions about the ad below.

1   (a) What pictures do you see on the product labels? _____

    (b) What do these pictures make you think of? _____

    _____

2. The ad uses these words to describe the products: fresh, farmer's market, and countryside. What main message does this ad want to send about the products?

    _____

3. What if the ad used these words: processed, packaged, and artificial? How would these words make you feel about the product? Why?

    _____

    _____

© Image courtesy of The Advertising Archives

HEALTH

Studies show that the best ads provide only a little information but create a lot of emotion. The emotion comes from the pictures and words in the ad. Some ads make you feel happy or remind you of a good experience in your life. If an ad makes you feel good, there is a better chance that you will buy the product.

Think again about the products in the ad on page 58.
Discuss the following questions. Give reasons for your answers.

▶▶ Discussion

4. How fresh are these products?

5. How healthy are these products?

6. What can you conclude about the actual product and what the ad wants us to believe about the product?

Analyze the ad below by discussing the following questions:

What is the main message the ad wants to send? Give reasons for your answer.

What can you conclude about the actual product and what the ad wants us to believe about the product?

© Image courtesy of The Advertising Archives

And what do you think?

One survey shows that 47% of people in Canada do not buy fresh fruit and vegetables. The main reason is that the prices are too high.

Source: Edmonton Journal, *Drastic price variation of healthy foods*, Feb. 2009.

Word Attack

Read the paragraph.
Circle five more words that have a suffix.

Before (starting) the meal, conscious (eaters) focus with a moment of silence, or a prayer. They think about where their food comes from. They think about and quietly thank the farmers who grow the food, and the people who pick, package, and deliver it.

Suffixes

Many words have more than one part. They have a base word and an end part.

start   start**ing**
eat   eat**ers**

The end part is called a **suffix.**

Read the paragraph.
Circle two compound words.

Conscious eaters sometimes lose weight because eating slowly allows them to notice when they are becoming full. Also, conscious eaters never eat just because they are bored or stressed. So conscious eaters do not overeat.

Compound Words

Compound words are made from two or more little words.

Read the sentences.
Divide the bolded words into parts.

Conscious eaters enjoy their feelings of **satisfaction**.

Conscious eaters **experiment** with new foods.

Conscious eaters try **different** recipes.

Divide and Conquer

Some words are hard to read because they are long. It is easier to read long words if you divide them into parts.

For example,

consciously   con / sci / ous / ly

Environment

Global Warming

Vocabulary: stabilize   convert   emit

Mini-Lesson: Cause and Effect

Literacy Practice: Diagram

Barbecue 2050

▶▶ **Discussion**

How important is the weather to you?
How often do you talk about the weather?
When do you pay attention to the weather? Why?

What groups of people pay a lot of attention to weather? Why?

Global warming is an important issue. What do you know about global warming?

What would you like to know about global warming? Write your questions here.

_____

_____

_____

_____

Read the passage to find out about global warming.

Global Warming

Have you ever seen a greenhouse? Most greenhouses look like small houses made of glass. The glass panels let in light and keep heat from escaping. The greenhouse heats up, just like a car parked in the sun with the windows closed.

© iStockphoto/EvansArtsPhotography

Many different gases surround the Earth. Some of these gases are called greenhouse gases. Greenhouse gases have the same effect on the Earth as glass on a greenhouse.

Stop and Think:

What effect do you think greenhouse gases have on the Earth? Read on to see if your ideas match the passage.

The sun's heat passes through the gases. The Earth's surface absorbs part of the heat. Part of the heat bounces back into outer space, and part of the heat is trapped by the greenhouse gases. The trapped heat that stays in the atmosphere causes the *greenhouse effect*. The greenhouse effect helps **stabilize** the Earth's temperature so that people, animals, and plants can survive.

Stop and Think:

What would happen if the greenhouse gases trapped too much heat?

Carbon dioxide (CO_2) and methane are two of the main greenhouse gases. They are produced in nature. For instance, trees absorb and **convert** CO_2 to oxygen. When trees die, they release their stored CO_2 into the atmosphere. All dying plants and animals release CO_2. Animals that eat hay and grass, such as cows and sheep, release methane gas as they digest food.

> **CO_2:** the scientific symbol for carbon dioxide. Carbon dioxide is made when carbon mixes with oxygen.

The greenhouse gases are getting thicker. They are trapping more and more heat. As a result, the Earth is warming up. This process is called global warming.

Why are the greenhouse gases getting thicker? The main reason is humans add a lot of extra carbon to the atmosphere. Burning fuel **emits** carbon. A car engine burns fuel, so driving a car produces carbon. Heating a home produces carbon. The process of generating electricity produces carbon. So every time we make coffee or turn on the TV, we add to global warming. The amount of carbon that we produce is called a *carbon footprint*. Our carbon footprint adds to global warming.

generate:
produce

Stop and Think:

How big is your carbon footprint?

Most scientists agree that global warming is a fact. Only two questions remain. How serious will the effects of global warming be? How will humans and animals adapt to the changes that are coming to the world they live in?

• • • • • • • • • • • • • • • •

Check the questions you wrote on page 61 about global warming. Did the information in the passage answer your questions?
   If not, where can you find the answers to your questions?

▶▶ Discussion

1. How does the size of your carbon footprint compare to the carbon footprint of people you know? How can you make your carbon footprint smaller?

2. Explain how the greenhouse effect works. Refer to the passage to check your ideas.

3. How are carbon dioxide and methane produced in nature? Find two examples.

4. Explain how the following add to global warming: (a) using a washing machine (b) eating a burger (c) using paper towels

5. Think about your community, city, or province. Who, or what, are the major producers of greenhouse gases? Who should be responsible for reducing these greenhouse gases? How can these greenhouse gases be reduced?

Vocabulary

Circle the best meaning for each bolded word.
Figure out what the word means by looking at how it is used in the sentence.

1. The thermostat in a fridge **stabilizes** the temperature. When the temperature inside the fridge warms up, the fridge turns on automatically.
   (a) cancels
   (b) decreases
   (c) freezes
   (d) holds steady

2. We can **convert** sunlight into electricity. This electricity is called solar power.
   (a) turn off and on
   (b) change from one thing into another
   (c) throw away
   (d) make bigger

3. A volcano **emits** soot, ash, and carbon when it erupts.
   (a) buries or hides
   (b) sends out; gives off
   (c) traps or stores
   (d) washes; makes free of germs

Write an answer for each question. Use complete sentences.

1. How do you **stabilize** a fever?

   _____

   _____

2. Why do some people **convert** from one religion to another?

   _____

   _____

3. Open sewers **emit** strong odours. What other things emit strong odours?

   _____

   _____

ENVIRONMENT

Dictionary Use

Use the dictionary entries to find the definition of the bolded word in each sentence.
Write the number of the definition beside each sentence.
The first one is an example.

> **pro-duce** (v.) **produced; producing 1:** to make something by using raw
> materials and machines *(produce cars)* **2:** to make something naturally *(bees
> produce honey)* **3:** to be the place where something comes from **4:** to be in
> charge of making a movie, TV show, etc. **5:** to show something when asked
> for it *(produce ID)* **6:** to give birth to

1. Saskatchewan **produces** wheat. __3__

2. The Hollywood star **produced** his first film last year. _____

3. Sugar maples **produce** sap. Sap is used to make maple syrup. _____

4. The tenant **produced** evidence of the landlord's neglect. _____

5. Female polar bears **produce** one to two cubs a year. _____

6. Factories **produce** steel. _____

> **e-mit** (v.) **emitted; emitting 1:** to send out heat, light, fumes, etc. from a certain
> source *(Chimneys emit smoke.)* **2:** to make (a sound) *(The furnace emits a
> loud noise.)*

7. Electric cars do not **emit** exhaust fumes. _____

8. The sun and stars **emit** light. _____

9. Old neon lights sometimes **emit** an odd buzzing noise. _____

Mini-Lesson: Cause and Effect

What is a cause and effect chain?

Good writers show the reader how their ideas are related to one another. Cause and effect is one way that ideas are related. Cause and effect relationships show how one thing makes something else happen. For example, it starts to snow, so the bus is late.

Cause	Effect
It starts to snow.	*The bus is late.*

Some cause and effect relationships are like a domino effect. One thing leads to another. The cause leads to Effect A. Effect A leads to Effect B, and so on. This domino effect is called a cause and effect chain.

Look at the following idea maps.
Add a possible effect to the cause and effect chain.

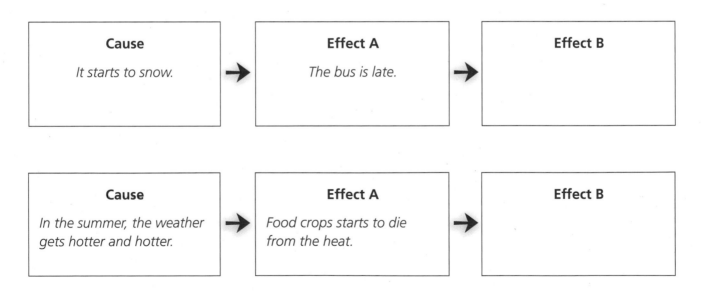

Active readers recognize how ideas relate to each other. Knowing how ideas relate to each other helps readers to understand the ideas.

Read the following paragraphs.
Finish the cause and effect idea maps.

Paragraph 1

The greenhouse gases are getting thicker. They are trapping more and more heat. As a result, the Earth is warming up. This process is called global warming.

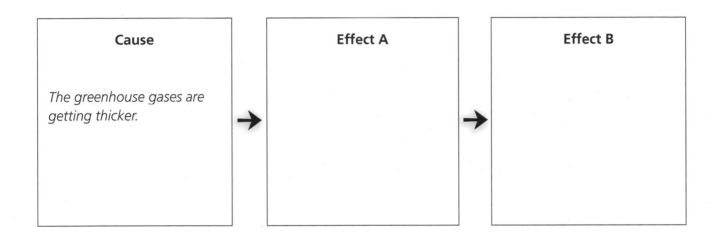

Cause	Effect A	Effect B
The greenhouse gases are getting thicker. →	→	

Paragraph 2

The trapped heat stays in the atmosphere. Heat in the atmosphere helps stabilize the Earth's temperature so that people, animals, and plants can survive.

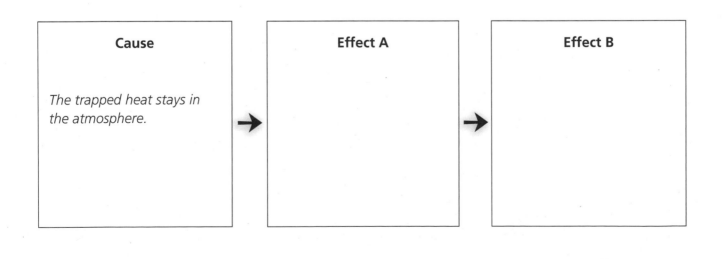

Cause	Effect A	Effect B
The trapped heat stays in the atmosphere. →	→	

Literacy Practice: Diagram

A diagram is worth a thousand words. Writers often use diagrams to help explain complex ideas. When reading a diagram, we must pay attention to the title, all the labels, and any symbols, such as arrows.

Answer the questions about the following diagram.

The Greenhouse Effect

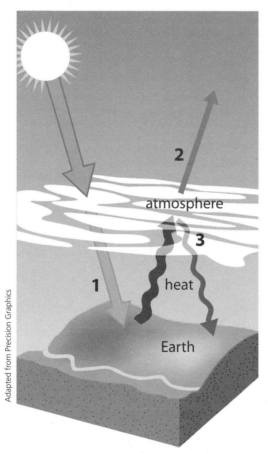

Adapted from Precision Graphics

1. What is the title of the diagram?

    _____

2. How many labels are used in the diagram?

    _____

3. What symbol is used to show the path of the sun's light and heat?

    _____

4. Match the numbers on the diagram to the sentences below.

    (a) _____ The sun's heat reaches the Earth.

    (b) _____ Some of the sun's heat bounces back into outer space.

    (c) _____ Some of the sun's heat is trapped in the atmosphere.

5. Sometimes the writer does not explain everything in a diagram. We need to figure some things out. Why do you think

    some arrows are squiggly?

    the arrows are different shades and thicknesses?

Answer the questions about the diagram on the following page.

The Carbon Cycle

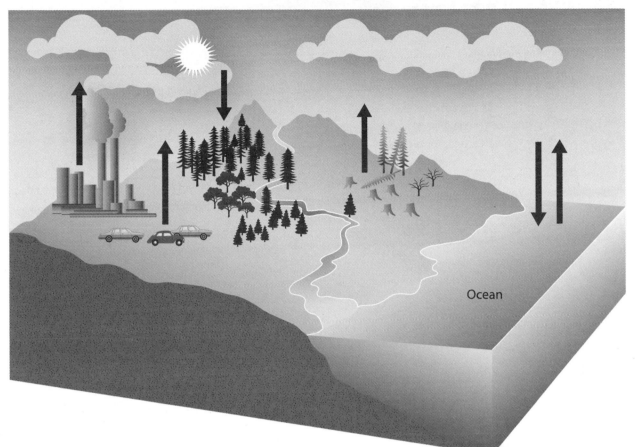

According to the diagram

1. What emits carbon into the atmosphere?

_____   _____   _____

2. What absorbs carbon from the atmosphere? _____

3. What both emits and absorbs carbon? _____

And what do you think?

About 30% of the world's land is used to grow feed for livestock rather than people.

Source: Food and Agriculture Organization of the United Nations (FAO).

Word Attack

Read the paragraph.
Circle eight more words that have a suffix.

The (sun's) heat (passes) through the gases.
The Earth's surface absorbs part of the heat.
Part of the heat bounces back into outer
space, and part of the heat is trapped by the
greenhouse gases. The trapped heat that stays
in the atmosphere causes the greenhouse
effect.

> **Suffixes**
>
> Many words have more than
> one part. They have a base
> word and an end part.
>
> sun   sun**'s**
> pass   pass**es**
>
> The end part is called a **suffix**.

Read the paragraph.
Circle two compound words.

Why are the greenhouse gases getting thicker?
The main reason is humans add a lot of
extra carbon to the atmosphere. Burning fuel
emits carbon. Generating electricity produces
carbon. The amount of carbon that we
produce is called a carbon footprint.

> **Compound Words**
>
> Compound words are made
> from two or more little words.

Read the sentences.
Divide the bolded words into parts.

Trapped heat in the **atmosphere** causes the
greenhouse effect.

The greenhouse effect helps stabilize the
Earth's **temperature**.

Carbon **dioxide** is a main greenhouse gas.

> **Divide and Conquer**
>
> Some words are hard to read
> because they are long. It is
> easier to read long words if
> you divide them into parts.
>
> For example,
>
> surround   sur / round

ENVIRONMENT

© iStockphoto/micheldenijs

Environment

Melting Ice

Vocabulary: expose   adapt   breed

Mini Lesson: Cause and Effect

Literacy Practice: Newspaper Article

WEIRD
WEATHER.

© www.CartoonStock.com/Ralph Hagen

▶▶ Discussion

Many scientists believe that climates around the world are changing. One cause of climate change is global warming.

Global warming is melting the Arctic ice. This thick sheet of ice is called a polar ice cap. People and animals in the Arctic depend on the polar ice cap for survival. What do you know about life in the Arctic and the melting ice cap?

What would you like to know about life in the Arctic and the melting ice cap? Write your questions here.

_____

_____

_____

_____

Read the passage to find out about the Arctic and the melting ice cap.

Melting Ice

The Arctic is home to polar bears. Antarctica is home to penguins. What do these lands have in common? Ice. And lots of it! Earth's polar ice caps are huge sheets of white ice. Hard white ice acts like a giant mirror that reflects sunlight and heat back into the atmosphere. The polar ice caps are the world's air conditioners.

© iStockphoto/ekvals

Stop and Think:

What happens to the world's temperature as the polar ice caps melt?

Global warming is melting the ice caps. As the ice caps melt, more of the ocean's surface is **exposed**. The dark ocean water absorbs the sun's heat and grows warmer. As more ocean water is exposed, more of the sun's heat is absorbed. So still more ice melts.

Polar bears depend on the Arctic ice for survival. Polar bears spend the winter raising their young and hunting on ice floes. The bears catch seals coming up to breathe through holes in the thick ice. But the ice floes are melting earlier in the spring, so the bears go hungry. Female polar bears lose weight and have fewer cubs. And fewer cubs are surviving. About 25,000 polar bears exist worldwide. Two thirds may disappear by the end of this century.

ice floe: a large sheet of free-floating sea ice

Stop and Think:

Why do you think fewer bear cubs are surviving?

The Inuit people struggle to **adapt** to changes caused by the melting ice. As the ice thins and shrinks, seals and polar bears change their feeding and migration habits. Finding seals and polar bears to hunt becomes more difficult. And the thin ice is preventing the Inuit from following their winter hunting routes.

migration: the movement of animals from one place to another at certain times of the year

ENVIRONMENT

Stop and Think:

Imagine you are a hunter in an Inuit community. What would you do to cope with the changes caused by the melting ice?

In Antarctica, Emperor penguins are dying. Krill, the penguins' main source of food, is decreasing due to melting ice. Emperor penguins used to march like ants across the ice to their breeding grounds. Now, the firm ice that the penguins **breed** on is shrinking and shifting. About 200,000 breeding pairs of Emperor penguins still live in Antarctica. If the ice keeps melting, up to 85 percent of these penguins may disappear by 2100.

Will all the ice melt? Not likely. But for now, humans and animals fight to adapt to the changing world of the polar ice caps.

krill: small sea animals that look like shrimp. Krill lay eggs in and eat the algae that grow on the underside of sea ice.

• • • • • • • • • • • • • •

Check the questions you wrote on page 71 about the Arctic and the polar ice caps. Did the information in the passage answer your questions? If not, where can you find the answers to your questions?

▶▶ Discussion

1. The melting ice will cause temperatures to change and sea levels to rise. How will this affect you and others around the world?

2. Find three reasons why the polar ice caps are important.

3. Are the melting ice caps affecting polar bears and penguins in the same way? Explain your answer.

4. How do you think the melting polar caps will affect the seal populations? Explain your answer.

5. What can people do to slow down climate change?

Vocabulary

Circle the best meaning for each bolded word.
Figure out what the word means by looking at how it is used in the sentence.

1. They took up the carpet and **exposed** the floor underneath it. They were surprised to find a beautiful hardwood floor.
   - (a) buried
   - (b) left without a cover or protection
   - (c) damaged
   - (d) covered up in order to hide

2. Seagulls live on beaches, in cities and dumps, and on farmland. Seagulls can **adapt** to different living conditions.
   - (a) fly around in
   - (b) move away from
   - (c) change behaviour to survive in
   - (d) get sick and die in

3. Rabbits **breed** quickly. A female rabbit can give birth to as many as 40 young a year.
   - (a) digest food
   - (b) move or hop
   - (c) die off
   - (d) produce young

Write an answer for each question. Use complete sentences.

1. We know that too much sun can cause skin problems. Why do you think some people continue to **expose** their bodies to the sun?

   _____

   _____

2. People **adapt** to new situations all the time. When was the last time you had to adapt to a new situation? Was it easy or hard to adapt? Explain why.

   _____

   _____

3. Mosquitoes **breed** in calm water. How can people reduce the number of mosquitoes?

   _____

   _____

Dictionary Use

Use the dictionary entries to find the definition of the bolded word in each sentence.
Write the number of the definition beside each sentence.
The first one is an example.

> **ex-pose** (v.) **exposed; exposing 1:** to leave something without cover or
> protection *(Colours fade if they are exposed to sunlight.)* **2:** to cause
> someone to experience and be affected by something *(My job exposes
> me to dangerous chemicals.)* **3:** to reveal something bad: UNCOVER
> *(expose a drug ring; expose a doctor as a quack)*

1. The lawyer **exposed** the woman as a liar and a thief. ___3___

2. Watching TV can **expose** children to a lot of violence. _____

3. Do not eat meat if it has been **exposed** to warm temperatures. _____

4. My grandfather **exposed** me to art when I was very young. _____

> **a-dapt** (v.) **1:** to change behaviour in order to survive in a place or situation **2:**
> to change something so that it works better or is more suitable *(The teacher
> adapted her teaching style to suit children.)* **3:** to change something so that
> it can be presented in another form *(a movie adapted from a book)*

5. The fitness instructor **adapted** the program to help seniors. _____

6. Children need time to **adapt** to a new school. _____

7. They **adapted** the knapsack so the dog could carry it. _____

8. The students wrote a play. The play was **adapted** from a poem. _____

Mini-Lesson: Cause and Effect

Some cause and effect relationships are like a domino effect. One thing leads to another. The cause leads to Effect A. Effect A leads to Effect B, and so on. This domino effect is called a cause and effect chain.

Look at the following idea map.
Add a possible effect to the cause and effect chain.

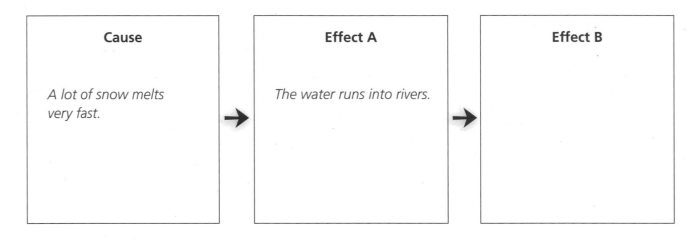

Cause		Effect A		Effect B
A lot of snow melts very fast.	→	*The water runs into rivers.*	→	

Read the following paragraphs. Finish the cause and effect idea maps.

Paragraph 1

As the ice thins and shrinks, seals and polar bears change their feeding and migration habits. Finding seals and polar bears to hunt becomes more difficult.

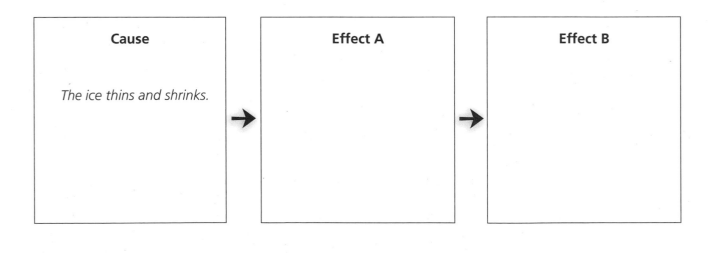

Cause		Effect A		Effect B
The ice thins and shrinks.	→		→	

Paragraph 2

The ice floes are melting earlier in the spring, so polar bears go hungry. Female polar bears lose weight and have fewer cubs.

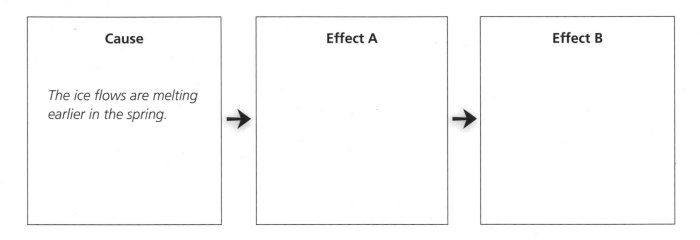

Cause	Effect A	Effect B
The ice flows are melting earlier in the spring.		

Paragraph 3

Krill is the penguins' main source of food. Krill is decreasing due to melting ice. Emperor penguins are dying.

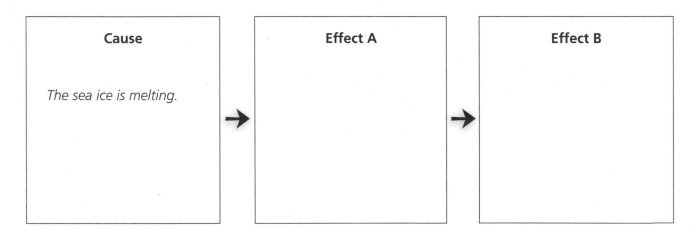

Cause	Effect A	Effect B
The sea ice is melting.		

Literacy Practice: Newspaper Article

People read newspapers for different reasons—for personal interest, to get the news, or for entertainment. Active readers preview a newspaper article and then decide if they want to read the rest of the article.

Previewing means getting an idea of the article's content. Previewing includes looking at pictures and captions, the headline, and straplines.

Previewing a newspaper article can also include reading the first paragraph. The first paragraph of a newspaper article tries to grab the reader's interest by introducing the key ideas in the article. The key ideas answer the questions who, what, where, when, why, and how.

The rest of the article provides more details about the key ideas.

Preview the newspaper article on the following page.
Then mark the following ideas as true (T) or false (F).

1. _____ A polar bear was shot.

2. _____ The polar bear was in Iqaluit.

3. _____ The students were in danger.

4. _____ The students were from a high school.

5. _____ The polar bear was a cub.

Are you interested in reading the rest of the newspaper article?
Read the question below. Add two more questions that the article might answer.

1. *Was anybody hurt?*

2. _____

3. _____

Now read the rest of the article.
As you read, look for answers to your questions.

Headline

Children run for cover before polar bear shot near Iqaluit

Strapline

Elementary students on picnic when wandering bear appears

A polar bear sent dozens of elementary school students racing for safety before the animal was shot and killed in a park just outside of Iqaluit on Wednesday.

At the time, 37 elementary students were in the park for a year-end picnic. Attempts to scare the bear away didn't work.

The officers and the RCMP at the scene said there was no choice but to kill the bear. There were too many people in the area. Summer visitors had set up about a dozen tents near the river.

A summer student working at the park said, "This is my first time seeing one here in the park. I was so amazed, and it's a huge, old male polar bear."

The bear was about 10 years old and

Polar bear wanders into local park.

Caption

about 2.5 m long. It seemed healthy and was likely looking for food in the park.

The bear's meat and skin were delivered to the office of the Iqaluit hunters and trappers association.

The students continued the picnic.

Source: Adapted from CBC News, June 25, 2008.

And what do you think?

Canada has a population of 33 million. South Africa has a population of 49 million. Canada uses three times more oil, natural gas, and electrical energy than South Africa.

Source: *World Resources Institute*, 2003.

Word Attack

Read the paragraph.
Circle nine more words that have a suffix.

(Polar)(bears) depend on the Arctic ice for survival. Polar bears spend the winter raising their young and hunting on ice floes. The bears catch seals coming up to breathe through holes in the thick ice. But the ice floes are melting earlier in the spring, so the bears go hungry.

Read the paragraph.
Circle the compound word.

Female polar bears lose weight and have fewer cubs. And fewer cubs are surviving. About 25,000 polar bears exist worldwide. Two thirds may disappear by the end of this century.

Read the sentences.
Divide the bolded words into parts.

Many polar bears may disappear by the end of the **century**.

Emperor penguins are dying.

The **Inuit** people struggle to adapt to changes caused by the melting ice.

Suffixes

Many words have more than one part. They have a base word and an end part.

pole   pol**ar**
bear   bear**s**

The end part is called a **suffix**.

Compound Words

Compound words are made from two or more little words.

Divide and Conquer

Some words are hard to read because they are long. It is easier to read long words if you divide them into parts.

For example,

Antarctica   Ant /.arc / ti / ca

ENVIRONMENT

© Grand-Pré National Historic Site of Canada

History
The Acadians

Vocabulary: thrive   self-sufficient   remote

Mini-Lesson: Chronological Order

Literacy Practice: Map

© Grand-Pré National Historic Site of Canada

Acadian Homes and Farms by Claude Picard

▶▶ Discussion

"I am Canadian." What does being Canadian mean to you?

Canada's identity has been shaped by many groups of people from many different places. The Acadians are one group of people who helped shape Canada's identity. The Acadians settled in Canada over 400 years ago.

What would you like to know about the Acadians? Write your questions here.

_____

_____

_____

_____

Read the passage to find the answers to your questions.

The Acadians

In 1604, the first French settlers landed in Acadia (present-day Nova Scotia). They settled in the Annapolis Valley. Life in this new land was hard. The winters were cold and the summers were short. Crops that grew in France did not do as well in the new land. Many French settlers died of malnutrition.

Ships Take Acadians into Exile by Claude Picard

The French settlers became known as the Acadians. Over the next 30 years, Acadian villages took root. The Mi'kmaq people showed the Acadians how to hunt and what to plant. Some Acadians married Mi'kmaq women. The two cultures came to respect each other.

Stop and Think:

What do you think "took root" means?

By the mid 1700s, about 13,000 Acadians lived in and around the Annapolis Valley. The Acadians' lives centred on family and community. Their farms were **thriving**. The Acadians owned over 100,000 cattle, a sign of their wealth. The Acadians had become **self-sufficient**. They did not want or need support from France to survive.

The Acadians had built good lives. But, life was about to change. Both Britain and France wanted to control North America. Britain gained control of the Annapolis Valley. The British wanted English-speaking people to settle in the Annapolis Valley. In 1754, the British asked the Acadians to take an oath of loyalty to Britain. Most Acadians did not want to take the oath of loyalty. They wanted to stay neutral. They did not want to be under British or French rule.

In 1755, the British began to deport the Acadians. The British burned the Acadians' farms and towns. They split up Acadian families. They loaded the Acadians like cattle onto ships.

The first Acadian Census took place in 1671. The total count was 392 people, 482 cattle, and 524 sheep.

oath: a serious and formal promise

deport: force people who are not citizens to leave a country

HISTORY

Stop and Think:

What do you think happened to the Acadians?
Read on to see if your ideas match the passage.

The British deported some Acadians to France. Many were sent south to the Thirteen Colonies. Some Acadians became slaves. Many died at sea. Some Acadian families found safety in the colony of Canada (present-day Quebec and Ontario). Between 1755 and 1763, the British removed about 75 percent of the Acadian people from their land.

Thirteen Colonies: the original 13 states of the United States

In 1764, the Acadians were allowed to return to Nova Scotia. The Acadians who returned did not get their farms and homes back. They settled in **remote** areas and rebuilt their lives. Many Acadians began to fish for a living. Acadians live in Nova Scotia today. They are a proud, strong people who continue to shape Canada's identity.

Stop and Think:

Imagine you were Acadian in 1764.
Would you return to Nova Scotia?
Why or why not?

• • • • • • • • • • • • • • • • • •

Check the questions you wrote on page 81 about the Acadians. Did the information in the passage answer your questions? What new questions did the passage make you think of?

▶▶ Discussion

1. What does the word identity mean to you? What words would you use to describe who you are? Describe the people and forces that helped shape your identity.

2. Did the British have a good enough reason to deport the Acadians? Support your opinion.

3. How did the British affect the Acadians' lives?

4. Life for the first French settlers—the original Acadians—was extremely hard. Why do you think they stayed in Acadia instead of returning to France?

5. Every year, thousands of newcomers arrive in Canada and the United States. What hardships do you think they face? What opportunities open up to them?

Vocabulary

Circle the best meaning for each bolded word.
Figure out what the word means by looking at how it is used in the sentence.

1. My son is **thriving** in his new school. He has new friends and better grades.
   (a) having serious difficulty
   (b) growing or developing with success
   (c) surviving, but just barely
   (d) doing too many things at once

2. She's **self-sufficient**. She has a good job and her own apartment.
   (a) selfish or uncaring
   (b) needing friends and family
   (c) without a job
   (d) able to live without help

3. There are not enough doctors who want to live and work in **remote** areas.
   (a) having good farmland
   (b) far away from cities
   (c) cool and dry
   (d) full of people

Write an answer for each question. Use complete sentences.

1. People **thrive** in different situations. Some people work well under stress. Other people are at their best when they feel needed. In what situations do you thrive?

_____

_____

2. In what ways are you **self-sufficient**? What helped you become self-sufficient?

_____

_____

3. Some people choose to live in areas far from other people and big city life. Describe one advantage and one disadvantage of living in a **remote** area.

_____

_____

Dictionary Use

Mark the following statements true (T) or false (F).
Use the dictionary entries as needed.

1. You should be able to depend on a person who makes a **vow**. _____

2. The Acadians were never **exiles**. _____

3. Acadian **descendants** live in Nova Scotia. _____

4. The British forced the Acadians to **disperse**. _____

---

disperse (v.) **dispersed; dispersing** to go or move in different directions: SPREAD APART *(The clouds dispersed after the rainstorm.)*

descendant (n.) **1:** someone who is related to a person or group of people who lived in the past **2:** something that developed from a thing that existed earlier *(Housecats are descendants of wild cats.)*

exile (n.) **1:** a time when a person is forced to live in another country *(He lived in exile for ten years.)* **2:** a person who is forced to live in another country

exile (v.) **exiled; exiling** to force someone to go live in another place: DEPORT

vow (n.) a serious promise to do something or act in a certain way: OATH *(wedding vows)*

vow (v.) to make a vow: PROMISE *(I vowed never to lie again.)*

Mini-Lesson: Chronological Order

Chronological order presents events in the order that they happened. Writers often use chronological order when they write about history or describe people's lives. Active readers recognize how ideas are organized. Knowing how ideas are organized helps readers to understand the ideas.

Read the following paragraph. Underline the chronological ideas as you read. Find the same chronological ideas on the timeline below.

Claude Picard

Claude Picard is a famous Acadian painter. He studied painting in Italy and France in the late 1950s. Picard loved to paint the beautiful countryside of his native New Brunswick. In 1986, Picard painted six murals in memory of the deportation of the Acadians. Picard received the Governor General's Medal in 1992 for his paintings. His paintings were displayed at the National Arts Centre in Ottawa in 1993. In 1996, a university in New Brunswick honoured Picard for his work in the arts.

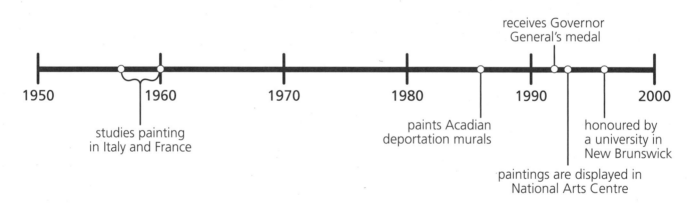

Use the timeline to answer the following questions:

1. What is the first year shown on the timeline? _____

2. What is the last year shown? _____

3. What is the total number of years shown on the timeline? _____

4. If the timeline were longer, what would be the year shown after the year 2000? _____

5. How are the late 1950s shown on the timeline? _____

Use the timeline below to answer the following questions:

1. What is the first year shown on the timeline? _____

2. What is the last year shown? _____

3. What is the total number of years represented on the time line? _____

4. What would be the next year shown on the timeline after the year 1765? _____

5. How many years did it take for Acadian settlements to take root? _____

6 (a) The Acadians arrived in 1604. About how many years did it take for the Acadians to become a thriving community? _____

   (b) Do you think this is a long time? Why or why not?

   _____

7. About how many years were the Acadians exiled? _____

8. What do you think the Acadians' life was like between 1635 and 1740?

   _____

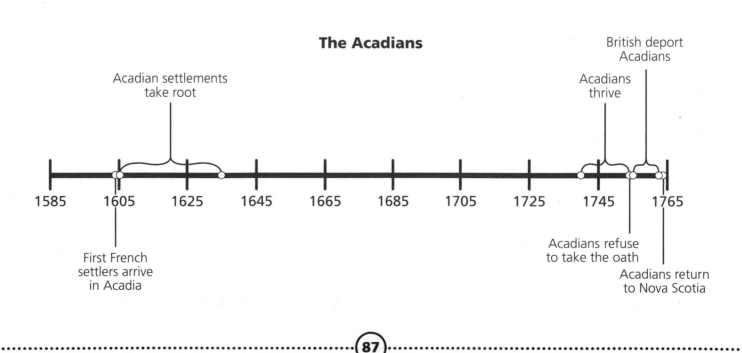

The Acadians

Acadian settlements take root

British deport Acadians

Acadians thrive

1585 1605 1625 1645 1665 1685 1705 1725 1745 1765

First French settlers arrive in Acadia

Acadians refuse to take the oath

Acadians return to Nova Scotia

Literacy Practice: Map

Maps provide a lot of information. They show the names and locations of places and bodies of water. They show direction and distance. And they show the size of cities and towns. When reading a map, pay attention to the title, any insets, the key, the compass, and the scale.

Answer the questions about the map on the following page.

Title

1. What is the title of the map? _____

2. What information does the title provide? _____

Inset

3. The small box in the inset shows Acadia's location in relation to Canada and the U.S. Where is Acadia located? Circle the correct answer.

    (a) on the west coast   (b) in central Canada   (c) on the east coast

Key

4. How many settlements are shown on the map? _____

5. How many forts are shown on the map? _____ Military bases? _____

6. Which country controlled the Magdalen Islands? _____

Compass

7. Find Ile Royale. Where is it located in relation to Halifax? Circle the correct answer.

    (a) west (b) south (c) northeast (d) southwest

Scale

8. What is the distance between Halifax and Louisbourg? Circle the correct answer.

    (a) less than 200 km   (b) 200 to 300 km   (c) over 300 km

    How did you figure out the answer?

9. Look at the settlements. Why do you think the Acadians settled in these places?

_____

10. Find one English name on the map. Find one French name on the map. Why do you think some places have English names and some places have French names?

_____

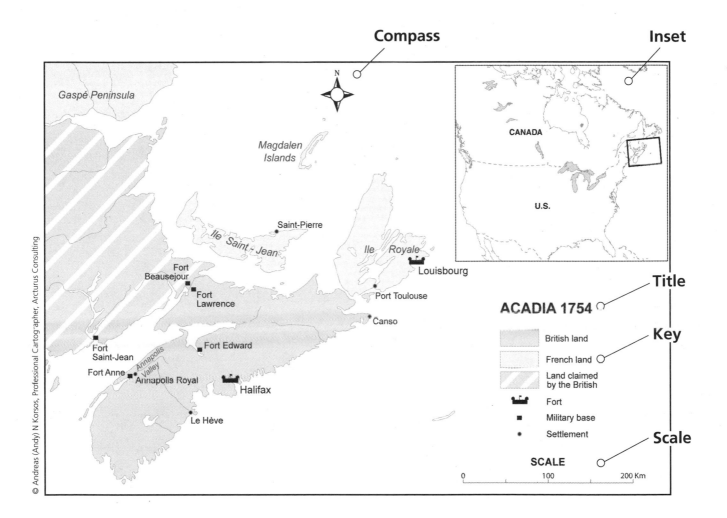

Compass

Inset

Gaspé Peninsula

N

CANADA

U.S.

Magdalen Islands

Saint-Pierre

Ile Saint-Jean

Ile Royale

Louisbourg

Fort Beausejour

Fort Lawrence

Port Toulouse

Canso

Fort Saint-Jean

Fort Edward

Fort Anne

Annapolis Valley

Annapolis Royal

Halifax

Le Hève

© Andreas (Andy) N Korsos, Professional Cartographer, Arcturus Consulting

Title

ACADIA 1754

Key

British land

French land

Land claimed by the British

Fort

Military base

Settlement

Scale

SCALE

0   100   200 Km

And what do you think?

Acadian Driftwood is a song about the Acadian experience, written by Canadian artist Robbie Robertson. The chorus begins with the lines

Acadian driftwood, gypsy tail wind
They call my home the land of snow…

Word Attack

Read the paragraph.
Circle six more words that have a suffix.

The British began to deport the (Acadians)
The British (burned) the Acadians' farms and
towns. They split up Acadian families. They
loaded the Acadians like cattle onto ships.

Read the paragraph.
Circle three words that have a prefix.

In 1764, the Acadians were allowed to
return to Nova Scotia. The Acadians who
returned did not get their farms and homes
back. They settled in remote areas and
rebuilt their lives.

Read the sentences.
Divide the bolded words into parts.

The French settlers became known as
Acadians.

Both Britain and France wanted to control
North **America.**

Some Acadian families found shelter in the
colony of Canada.

Suffixes

Many words have more than
one part. They have a base
word and an end part.

Acadian   Acadian**s**
burn   burn**ed**

The end part is called a **suffix.**

Prefixes

Many words have more than
one part. They have a base
word and a beginning part.

nutrition   **mal**nutrition
port   **de**port

The beginning part is called a
prefix.

Divide and Conquer

Some words are hard to read
because they are long. It is
easier to read long words if
you divide them into parts.

For example,

Annapolis   An / na / pol / is

© Library of Congress Prints and
Photographs Division, 08370u

History
Settling the Prairies

Vocabulary: potential   isolation   prosperous

Mini-Lesson: Chronological Order

Literacy Practice: Line Graph

© Glenbow Archives NA-449-3

Settlers camped on Grande Prairie Trail, Alberta

▶▶ Discussion

In the late 1800s, settlers came from
other countries to settle in the Canadian
prairies.

What do you know about the settlers
who came to the Canadian prairies?
What would you like to know about
these settlers? Write your questions here.

_____

_____

_____

_____

Read the passage to find the answers to
your questions.

Settling the Prairies

By 1885, Canada's national dream had come true. A railway stretched from coast to coast. It had taken ten years for 12,000 men, 5,000 horses, and 300 dog-sled teams to build the railway across Canada. The western prairies were now open to settlement.

© Library of Congress Prints and Photographs Division, 08370u

The government wanted to fill the land with farmers and ranchers. Canada took serious steps to attract settlers to the prairies. Canada offered free and cheap land to **potential** settlers. Canada sent agents to Britain, Europe, and the United States. The agents held meetings in town halls. They went to trade fairs.

Agents described the prairies as a land of milk and honey. The settlers were told that turnips grew to 30 pounds and carrots to 11 pounds. The agents said the winters were dry and pleasantly cool. Agents did not mention the summer mosquitoes, winter blizzards, and grapes that looked more like raisins. They did not talk about the **isolation** of life on the prairie.

the prairies: large areas of flat grassland found in the provinces of Manitoba, Alberta, and Saskatchewan

Stop and Think:

What problems do you think the settlers faced when they arrived on the prairies?
Read on to see if your ideas match the passage.

The settlers arrived. Some were disappointed and left, but most stayed. Life on the prairies was an improvement over what many had left behind. Still, for these first settlers, prairie life was difficult. The prairie grassland was rich and fertile but hard to till. Grain crops that grew in milder climates did not grow as well on the prairies. Crops failed and people went hungry.

fertile: having rich soil that is good for growing

till: prepare a piece of land for growing crops

Settlers used sod, rather than wood, to construct their simple homes. Sod was cut from the ground and stacked like bricks to form walls. Most floors in the sod houses were packed dirt. Windows were a luxury. The sod houses were simple, but they kept out heat in the summer and bitter cold in the winter.

sod: the top layer of soil that is made from grass and plant roots

Stop and Think:

Why do you think the settlers used sod rather than wood to build their homes?

The settlers suffered hardships, but many wrote home saying that life was good in Canada. More settlers came, and the prairies filled with people from different countries. Towns and cities grew. Many farmers who started out poor became **prosperous**.

Stop and Think:

Imagine you are a settler. Life is hard in your new home. Why do you write home saying life is good?

In less than a generation, more than two million people called the prairies home. These early settlers helped turned the prairies into the breadbasket of Canada. These early settlers helped build a nation.

breadbasket:
a region that grows lots of grains such as wheat or barley

Check the questions you wrote on page 91 about the settlers. Did the information in the passage answer your questions? What new questions did the passage make you think of?

▶▶ Discussion

1. What would make you leave your home country to start a new life in another country?

2. How well did the Canadian government prepare and support the first settlers for life in the prairies? Very well? Somewhat well? Not at all? Explain your answer.

3. In what ways was life hard for the settlers on the prairies?

4. Why did the agents describe the prairies as a land of milk and honey?

5. Canada is home to people from all over the world. In your opinion, what are Canadians' attitudes toward newcomers? How are people's attitudes toward newcomers shaped?

Vocabulary

Circle the best meaning for each bolded word.
Figure out what the word means by looking at how it is used in the sentence.

1. The new drug will help people who are depressed. Doctors say the drug also has other **potential** benefits.
   (a) negative   (b) expensive
   (c) possible   (d) unhealthy

2. The old couple lived in **isolation** on the little island. They had no phone. They rowed their boat to the nearest village once a year to buy supplies.
   (a) a crowded place   (b) history; life story
   (c) fear of being alone   (d) separation from others

3. The business had a **prosperous** year. All the employees got big raises.
   (a) having success by making money   (b) full of problems
   (c) usual; having nothing new   (d) up and down; not predictable

Write an answer for each question. Use complete sentences.

1. Moving into a new community is like an adventure. There are **potential** problems as well as pleasant surprises. What is one pleasant surprise you might find in a new community?

_____

_____

2. People often live in **isolation** in their own communities. They do not speak to or even know their neighbours. How can individuals help to build community?

_____

_____

3. Different areas of a big city grow in different ways. Why do some areas of a city grow to be more **prosperous** than other areas of the same city?

_____

_____

HISTORY

Dictionary Use

**Mark the following statements true (T) or false (F).
Use the dictionary entries as needed.**

1. A warm climate would **lure** tourists. _____

2. **Pioneers** never leave their place of birth. _____

3. You should vote for a government that uses **propaganda**. _____

4. It is impossible to sell a **homestead**. _____

5. Settlers from Europe **homesteaded** the Canadian prairies. _____

---

homestead (n.) **1:** a house and the farmland it is on **2:** a piece of public land offered to a settler by the government in order to develop the land

homestead (v.) to settle on government land and farm it

lure (n.) **1:** an attractive quality *(the lure of job opportunities)* **2:** a thing used to attract animals *(Worms are used as live fishing lures.)*

lure (v.) **lured; luring** to convince a person or animal to go somewhere or do something by promising some kind of pleasure or gain: ATTRACT *(He lured the cat from under the bed with a toy mouse.)*

propaganda (n.) false ideas that are spread in a planned way to help a cause, a political leader, a government *(Ads are often nothing but propaganda.)*

pioneer (n.) **1:** a person who helps create or develop new ideas or ways of doing things: INVENTOR *(They were pioneers in the field of computer technology.)* **2:** someone who is one of the first people to move into and live in a new area

pioneer (v.) to help create or develop new ideas or ways of doing things

---

Mini-Lesson: Chronological Order

Chronological order presents events in the order that they happened. Writers often use chronological order when they write about history.

Read the following passage. Then fill in the missing events on the timeline on the following page.

Building the Railway in Canada

The first railway in Canada was built **in 1836** in the Maritime colonies. **In 1855,** a railway line opened connecting Toronto and Montreal. **By 1860,** the railway companies were deep in debt. They started to cut costs. The government passed a law **the same year** to make sure the cuts in cost did not affect the safety of passengers.

© Glenbow Archives NA-990-3

In 1867, New Brunswick and Nova Scotia joined Quebec and Ontario to form the new country of Canada. But there was a condition. New Brunswick and Nova Scotia wanted a railway to connect the Maritimes to Quebec. Many little railways were built in the Maritimes **during the 1870s.** The main railway in the Maritimes was finished **in 1876.**

British Columbia joined Canada **in 1871.** British Columbia also wanted to be joined to the rest of Canada by rail. **In 1875,** the Canadian Pacific Railway (CPR) started to build the main part of the national railway. On **November 7, 1885,** the last railway spike was put in place. The railway now linked Canada from east to west. Canada's national railway was born.

Building the Railway in Canada

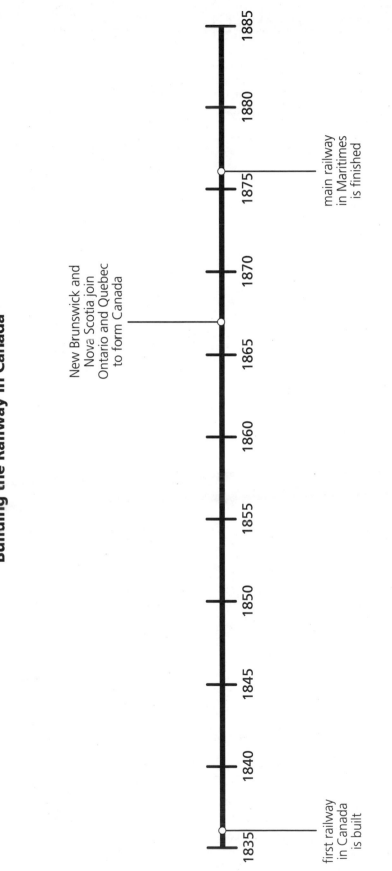

1835 — first railway in Canada is built

1840

1845

1850

1855

1860

1865

1867 — New Brunswick and Nova Scotia join Ontario and Quebec to form Canada

1870

1875 — main railway in Maritimes is finished

1880

1885

Literacy Practice: Line Graph

Line graphs show a lot of information, or data, using few words. We use line graphs to show how things change over time. When reading a line graph, we must pay attention to the title, the two axes, any text, and the lines in the graph. The lines in the graph represent the data.

Use the line graph to answer the questions on the following page.

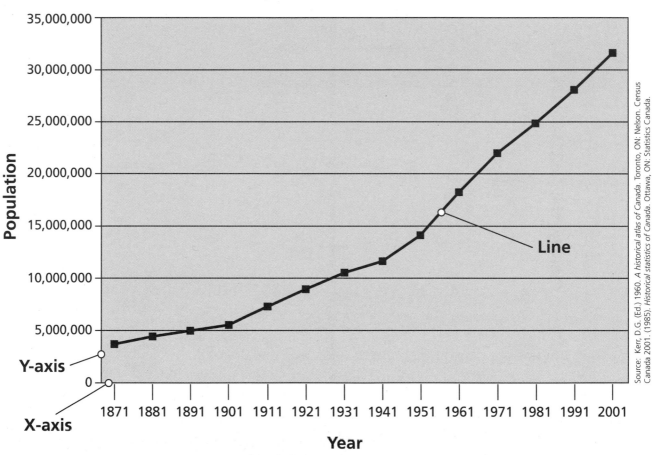

Source: Kerr, D.G. (Ed.) 1960. *A historical atlas of Canada*. Toronto, ON: Nelson. Census Canada 2001. (1985). *Historical statistics of Canada*. Ottawa, ON: Statistics Canada.

Text — In the early years of the 1900s, over 20 percent (1 in 5) of people in Canada were newcomers. But the number of newcomers arriving in Canada dropped during the Great Depression (1930s) and World War II (1939–1945). After World War II, the government began to invite more newcomers into Canada to make sure Canada's population would keep growing.

1. What is the title of the line graph? _____

2. The X-axis shows years. What would the next number on the X-axis be? _____

3. What does the Y-axis show? _____

4. The range of the Y-axis is from 0 to 35,000,000. What would the next number on the Y-axis be? _____

5. The line graph has one line. What does the line represent?

   _____

6. At what year does the line start? _____ At what year does the line end? _____

7. The line on the graph goes up. What does this tell us about Canada's population from 1871 to 2001?

   _____

8. Where did the information for the line graph come from?

   (a) a historical atlas of Canada   (c) a census of Canada

   (b) Statistics Canada   (d) a, b, and c

9. Why is it important to know the source of information?

   _____

10. When did the population of Canada increase the most?

   (a) from 1871 to 1901   (b) from 1901 to 1941   (c) from 1951 to 2001

   (b) Why did the population increase during this time?

   _____

And what do you think?

Canada was one of many countries that did not accept Jewish refugees during World War II. In 1967, Canada began to accept newcomers based on skills, education, and language rather than race.

Word Attack

Read the paragraph.
Circle four more words that have a suffix.

The (settlers) (arrived.) Some were disappointed and left, but most stayed. Life on the prairies was an improvement over what many had left behind. Still, for these first settlers, prairie life was difficult.

> **Suffixes**
>
> Many words have more than one part. They have a base word and an end part.
>
> settle   settle**rs**
> arrive   arrive**d**
>
> The end part is called a **suffix.**

Read the paragraph.
Circle two compound words.

The prairie grassland was rich and fertile but hard to till. Grain crops that grew in milder climates did not grow as well on the prairies. Crops failed and people went hungry. And yet, these early settlers helped turn the prairies into the breadbasket of Canada.

> **Compound Words**
>
> Compound words are made from two or more little words.

Read the sentences.
Divide the bolded words into parts.

The government passed a law to protect the safety of **passengers**.

Agents did not mention the summer **mosquitoes**, winter blizzards, and grapes that looked more like raisins.

In less than a **generation**, more than two million people called the prairies home.

> **Divide and Conquer**
>
> Some words are hard to read because they are long. It is easier to read long words if you divide them into parts.
>
> For example,
>
> Canadian   Ca / nad / i / an

In some cases, the answer key contains only a few of the possible responses for the discussion questions.

People

Unit 1. Susan Aglukark

Discussion: 1. Student responses will vary. **2.** Susan sang and played guitar as a young girl. Her music made her famous. She sings about her life. She spends a lot of time on her music. Her music took her to Ontario. **3.** She sings songs about the Inuit people that give them hope. She works with youth at risk. She acts as a mentor to young artists. She speaks about social issues. She teaches Native Studies. She lobbies the government in support of the Aboriginal people. **4.** Her father was a minister. She went through hard times in life and looked to her faith to help her. **5.** Student responses will vary.

Vocabulary: 1. d **2.** b **3.** a

Dictionary: 1. 3 **2.** noun/verb **3.** lobbies **4.** 1

Mini-Lesson: (p. 6) Possible responses: **1.** I think some kids were bullying him because kids can be cruel when they're young. **2.** I think someone broke into a car because a lot of robberies take place in the middle of the night. **(p. 7)** Possible responses: **1.** I think Susan didn't have confidence in her ability to sing. **2.** I think Susan cares about the future of her people. **3.** I think Susan realizes how important education is. **4.** I think Susan has to live in Ontario because there is more work for her there than in her home community.

Literacy Practice: 1. Top Reasons for Going to College **2.** 28,932 **3.** 10: The bars represent the percentage of students who chose each reason. **4.** from most common reason to least common reason **5.** percentage of students from 0% to 100% **6.** Human Resources and Skills Development Canada **7.** 2007 (The data might have been collected earlier and not published until 2007.) **8.** Possible response: survey by phone or mail **9.** Possible responses: There may have been errors made when the data was being organized. The data may be outdated. Respondents do not tell the truth all the time on surveys. The survey questions may have encouraged respondents to answer in a certain way. **10.** getting a job **11.** helping decide on a career **12.** 56 **13.** 45 **14.** 41 **15.** Student responses will vary.

Word Attack: Suffixes: started / singing / communities / trained / loved / dreamed
Compound Words: everything / everyone / ourselves **Divide and Conquer:** Student responses will vary.

Unit 2: Bill Reid

Discussion: 1. Student responses will vary. **2.** having multicultural parents, studying jewellery-making, studying Haida designs, seeing the bracelets his uncle had made, working on Haida totem poles **3.** He used Haida designs in his jewellery-making. He spent time working on Haida totem poles. He wanted to show the world the culture of the Haida people. **4.** Possible responses: Bill is respected as an artist. The government wanted to honour Bill's work. **5.** Student responses will vary.

Vocabulary: 1. c **2.** d **3.** a

Dictionary: 1. 4 **2.** noun, verb **3.** 3 **4.** 2 **5.** adjective **6.** The news about her mother was stunning. Student responses will vary regarding what the news may be.

Mini-Lesson: (p.16) Possible responses: **1.** I think Bill was creative as a child because he used everyday items to create art. **2.** I think Bill moved back to Vancouver because he wanted to be near his family and community. **3.** I think Bill was proud of his culture and people because he wanted to tell the world about them. **4.** I think the *The Raven and the First Men* was a complicated sculpture because it took so long to finish. **(p.17)** Possible inferences: Jen's grandmother loved nature. Jen's grandmother lived in a warm climate.

Literacy Practice: (p.18) 1. flags **2.** Possible response: We are sad when one person dies, but we don't care if thousands of people die. **3.** to send a message or create an emotion **4.** Student responses will vary. **5.** We have become hardened to the fact that so many people are killed in wars or conflict. We only care if someone we know dies. **6.** people who have lost someone in a war; war veterans; people who live in a place where many are dying because of hunger, disease, or oppression **(p. 19)** Student responses will vary.

Word Attack: Suffixes: trees / repairing / poles / carving / ones / Bill's / treasures / started / making / sculptures **Compound Words:** workshop **Divide and Conquer:** Student responses will vary.

Relationships

Unit 3. Conflict Styles

Discussion: 1. Student responses will vary. **2.** Our Way is the most positive style because it is collaborative. Both partners have equal say and the solution is more stable than a quick fix. **3.** avoiding the problem, not having a chance to express your thoughts and emotions, ignoring your needs, losing your temper, yelling, not listening to the other person **4.** Possible responses: by making conflict an opportunity to learn about yourself and your partner, communicate with your partner, or grow closer to your partner **5.** Student responses will vary.

Vocabulary: 1. c **2.** a **3.** c

Dictionary: 1. It is easier to remember how to spell long words. **2.** Student responses will vary **3.** collaborated **4.** cooperate

Mini-Lesson: (p. 26) 1. costs time and money to clean up, makes the city look bad and rundown **2.** The writer is against graffiti. **(p. 27)** Student responses will vary.

Literacy Practice: Letter 1: 1. the hairdresser and the hairdresser's friend **2.** The hairdresser's friend wants a free haircut and meal. The hairdresser wants to keep her friend but does not want to give free haircuts and pay for dinner all the time. **3.** Your Way (give in and keep the peace) **4.** Student responses will vary. **Letter 2: 1.** a husband and his wife **2.** Possible responses: The husband wants to understand his wife and make her happy. He wants his wife to stop criticizing him and being so demanding. The wife wants her husband to change. She wants attention. **3.** Your Way (give in and keep the peace) or Walk Away (does not want to argue) **4.** Student responses will vary.

Word Attack: Suffixes: values / beliefs / disagreeing / sorts / things / disagreements / called / conflicts / different / ways **Compound Words:** something / halfway **Divide and Conquer:** Student responses will vary.

Unit 4: Active Listening

Discussion: 1. Student responses will vary. **2.** the speaker, the speaker's words, the speaker's tone of voice, the speaker's pace of words **3.** to encourage the speaker to talk openly, to ask questions in order to understand the speaker's message, to confirm what the speaker means, to sum up the speaker's main points, to give feedback or advice **4.** Possible responses: Active listening leads to both people knowing each other better, which means growing closer to each other. Growing close to a person involves trusting the person. / When a person knows someone really listens all the time, the person will speak more openly. This means trusting the listener. **5.** Student responses will vary.

Vocabulary: 1. a **2.** a **3.** c

Dictionary: 2a. paraphrased **2b.** paraphrasing **3.** restate **5.** 2, set up, prove

Mini-Lesson: (p. 36) Student responses will vary. **(p. 37) 1.** a classic education; daycare centres; safety; meal programs; teaching of values, choices, and self-esteem **2.** enough education to get a job

Literacy Practice: Student responses will vary.

Word Attack: Suffixes: involved / listening / listener / speaker / improved / relationships / parts / lives **Compound Words:** sometimes / feedback **Divide and Conquer:** Student responses will vary.

Health

Unit 5. Why Vegetarian?

Discussion: 1. Student responses will vary. **2.** Pigs are better because they produce less manure **3.** Factory farms are cruel to animals. / Factory farms need a lot of land to raise and feed the animals. This land could be used to produce grain for people to eat. / Factory farms can pollute drinking water. / Factory farms add to global warming by using fossil fuels. **4.** Possible responses: These products come from animals. These animals may be raised in factory farms. **5.** Student responses will vary.

Vocabulary: 1. c **2.** a **3.** b

Dictionary: b. understand **c.** receive **2.** 4 **3.** 3 **4.** 2 **5.** 1. **6.** 2 **7.** 4

Mini-Lesson: (p. 47) Topic: b **Main idea:** Protein is important. **Supporting details:** helps build muscles, blood, skin, hair, nails, and organs; helps blood clot; helps metabolism; helps bodies fight off disease

Literacy Practice: (p. 48) a. 3 **b.** 5 **c.** 1 **d.** 4 **e.** 2

	Whole Wheat Bread	Peanut Butter (Kraft)
What is the serving size?	2 slices (64 g)	1 tbsp (15 g)
How many calories are in the serving?	140	90
How many grams (g) of fat are in the serving?	1.5	8
How many grams of protein are in the serving?	5	3

(p. 49) 1. Bread is healthier. It has less fat and more protein. **2.** 8 g (2 slices bread + peanut butter) **3.** No. Peanut butter has a lot of fat. It is healthier to get protein from many different foods.

Word Attack: Suffixes: handled / farms / lots / fuels / burning / leads / global / warming
Compound Words: pastureland / wildlife **Divide and Conquer:** Student responses will vary.

Unit 6. Conscious Eaters

Discussion: 1. Student responses will vary. **2.** Yes. Before they start eating, they take time to have a moment of silence, pray, or think about their food. They take small bites and chew the food many times. They pause between mouthfuls. They take time over the last bite. They relax and breathe after finishing the meal. They take time to enjoy their feelings of satisfaction. **3.** becoming a healthier eater, discovering new foods, losing weight, not overeating **4.** Possible responses: Eating slowly, chewing food carefully, being relaxed while eating, and not overeating all help the stomach digest food easily. **5.** Student responses will vary.

Vocabulary: 1. b **2.** d **3.** d

Dictionary: 2. 3 **3.** 2 **4.** 1 **5.** 2 **6.** 1

Mini-Lesson: Paragraph 1: Topic: c **Main idea:** Conscious eaters eat slowly. **Paragraph 2: Topic:** b **Main idea:** Growing rice is not easy work. **Paragraph 3: Topic:** a **Main idea:** Eating slowly helps digest food.

Literacy Practice: 1a. bowl of soup, vegetables **1b.** Possible responses: eating fresh vegetables, preparing home cooked meals, growing a garden, living on a farm, the outdoors, healthy living **2.** The products are healthy or organic, grown naturally on a farm, and freshly picked. **3.** Student responses will vary. **4.** The food is not very fresh. It may have been picked before it was ripe. It has been processed and packaged. It took time, maybe days, to get it to the food-processing factory. **5.** The food is not as healthy as the ad suggests. It may have artificial colouring and preservatives in it, or lots of salt and fat. It may have been grown in soil that has chemicals in it. The food might have a low content of good things like fibre, protein, minerals, and vitamins. **6.** There is little connection between the actual product and the ad's message. The products are not as healthy and fresh as the ad wants us to believe.

Word Attack: Suffixes: prayer / comes / quietly / farmers / package **Compound Words:** sometimes / overeat **Divide and Conquer:** Student responses will vary.

Environment

Unit 7. Global Warming

Discussion: 1. Possible responses: use less electricity; recycle, reuse, reduce; walk or bike instead of driving or taking the bus **2.** The greenhouse gases include carbon dioxide and methane. These gases trap some of the sun's heat in the atmosphere. The trapped heat stabilizes the Earth's temperature so that living things can survive. Without the greenhouse effect, the Earth's temperature would decrease a lot. **3.** Dying trees give off carbon. Dying plants and animals give off carbon. Animals that eat hay and grass release methane gas. **4.** Possible responses: **a.** Washing clothes uses electricity. Using electricity adds to global warming. **4b.** The meat for hamburgers comes from cattle. Cattle emit methane. / Cattle require pastureland, which means cutting down forests. Dead trees emit carbon dioxide. **4c.** Paper comes from trees. Using paper towels means fewer trees to absorb carbon dioxide. **5.** Student responses will vary.

Vocabulary: 1. d **2.** b **3.** b

Dictionary: 2. 4 **3.** 2 **4.** 5 **5.** 6 **6.** 1 **7.** 1 **8.** 1 **9.** 2

Mini Lesson: (p. 67) Paragraph 1: Effect A: They are trapping more and more heat. **Effect B:** The Earth is warming up. **Paragraph 2: Effect A:** The heat helps stabilize the Earth's temperature. **Effect B:** People, animals, and plants can survive.

Literacy Practice: (p. 68) 1. The Greenhouse Effect **2.** 3 **3.** arrow **4a.** 1 **b.** 2 **c.** 3 **5.** The squiggly arrows show heat that has bounced off something. The different shades and thicknesses show different intensities of heat. **(p. 69) 1.** factories, cars, dying trees **2.** living trees **3.** the ocean

Word Attack: Suffixes: gases / Earth's / absorbs / bounces / outer / trapped / stays / causes
Compound Words: greenhouse / footprint **Divide and Conquer:** Student responses will vary.

Unit 8. Melting Ice

Discussion: 1. Student responses will vary. **2.** The polar ice caps are home to people and animals. They keep the Earth cool. **3.** Yes. The melting ice caps are affecting the diet and breeding patterns of both polar bears and penguins. Also, both polar bears and penguins are in danger of disappearing. **4.** Because of the melting ice, it is harder for hunters and polar bears to find the seals. So, the seal population might increase. **5.** Possible answer: reduce carbon footprint by recycling, reusing, and reducing

Vocabulary: 1. b **2.** c **3.** d

Dictionary: 2. 2 **3.** 1 **4.** 2 **5.** 2 **6.** 1 **7.** 2 **8.** 3

Mini-Lesson: (p. 76) Paragraph 1: Effect A: Seals and polar bears change their habits. **Effect B:** Finding seals and polar bears to hunt becomes more difficult. **Paragraph 2: Effect A:** Polar bears go hungry. **Effect B:** Female polar bears lose weight and have fewer cubs. **Paragraph 3: Effect A:** Krill is decreasing. **Effect B:** Emperor penguins are dying.

Literacy Practice: 1. T **2.** F **3.** T **4.** F **5.** F

Word Attack: Suffixes: survival / raising / hunting / floes / seals / coming / holes / melting / earlier
Compound Words: worldwide **Divide and Conquer:** Student responses will vary.

History

Unit 9: The Acadians

Discussion: Possible responses: **1.** Identity means who you are, how you see or feel about yourself, and how you got to be the person you are. **2.** No. The Acadians were peaceful. They were developing the land. They did not take the oath of loyalty, but this is not a reason to deport them. **3.** The Acadians lost their homes, were separated from their families, and suffered or died because of the British. The Acadians had to rebuild their lives in new places. **4.** Possible responses: The Mi'kmaq helped the Acadians survive. Some Acadians married Mi'kmaq women. Their farms began to thrive. Life was better for them in Acadia than in France. The French government wanted them to stay so that the land would belong to France, not Britain. The Acadians were strong and determined people. **5.** Student responses will vary.

Vocabulary: 1. b **2.** d **3.** b

Dictionary: 1. T **2.** F **3.** T **4.** T

Mini-Lesson: (p. 86) 1. 1950 **2.** 2000 **3.** 50 **4.** 2010 **5.** with a semi-circle spanning the years from 1957 to 1959 **(p. 87) 1.** 1585 **2.** 1765 **3.** 180 **4.** 1785 **5.** 30 **6a.** about 135 **6b.** Student responses will vary.
7. about 9 **8.** Possible responses: They lived peacefully with the Mi'kmaq. They worked hard to survive and develop their farms. They lived a simple life. They minded their own business.

Literacy Practice: 1. Acadia 1754 **2.** the year and the place that the map focuses on **3.** c **4.** 5 **5.** 2, 5 **6.** France **7.** northeast **8.** b **9.** Possible responses: The settlements are on the coast so they are easy to get to by water. The Acadians can fish. **10.** Possible responses: The French and British were fighting for control. Some places were controlled by the French and some by the British.

Word Attack: Suffixes: Acadians' / farms / towns / families / loaded / ships **Prefixes:** return / returned / rebuilt (Note: The "re" in remote is not a suffix.) **Divide and Conquer:** Student responses will vary.

Unit 10. Settling the Prairies

Discussion: 1. Student responses will vary. **2.** Possible response: Not at all. The government offered free or cheap land to the settlers, but the government did not tell the settlers the truth about life on the prairies. When the settlers arrived, they had to cope the best they could. **3.** The winters were freezing cold with blizzards. There were lots of mosquitoes in the summer. The land was hard to till. Crops were hard to grow. People went hungry. There was no wood to build homes. **4.** Canada needed people to settle in the prairies, so the agents made the prairies sound like a beautiful place to live. **5.** Student responses will vary.

Vocabulary: 1. c **2.** d **3.** a

Dictionary: 1. T **2.** F **3.** F **4.** F **5.** T

Mini-Lesson: (p. 97) Complete timeline with following dates and events: 1855: railway connects Toronto and Montreal / 1860: railway companies cut costs / 1860: law passed to protect passengers / 1870s: many railways built in Maritimes / 1871: British Columbia joins Canada / 1875: CPR starts to build main part of railway / 1885: railway is finished

Literacy Practice: 1. Population of Canada **2.** 2011 **3.** population **4.** 40,000,000 **5.** how the population of Canada has changed **6.** 1871, 2001 **7.** The population increased. **8.** d **9.** Knowing the source of information helps you decide how reliable or true the information is. **10a.** c **10b.** After WWII, the government of Canada began to invite newcomers into Canada.

Word Attack: Suffixes: disappointed / stayed / prairies / improvement **Compound Words:** grassland / breadbasket **Divide and Conquer:** Student responses will vary.